The Girl from Rector's

The Girl from Rector's

George Rector

COACHWHIP PUBLICATIONS
GREENVILLE, OHIO

The Girl from Rector's, by George Rector
© 2024 Coachwhip Publications edition

First published 1927
George Rector, 1878-1947
CoachwhipBooks.com

ISBN 1-61646-594-8
ISBN-13 978-1-61646-594-0

CONTENTS

Chapter 1   9
The Man Who Changed Broadway—Please Step into My Parlor—Change Partners—Painting the Lily

Chapter 2   17
Dan Daly's Escargots—Diamond Jim's Lighting System—An Earnest Eater—Oysters in Tin Shells—Tea Time at the World's Fair—A Restaurant Gridiron—Another Round-Tripper

Chapter 3   31
Evaporation of Silverware—A Hot Time in the Old Town—Ali Rabit's Luxury—My, 'Twas a Hansom Parade!—The Divine Sarah in an Earthly Role—On the Trail of Sauce Marguery—Prunes Wrong End To

Chapter 4   45
Cooking in a Foreign Language—Jumping on the Grapes—Chef and Guest of Honour—The Café de Paris Crown Jewel—A Cure for an Epicure—Sauce for the Geese

Chapter 5   57
　Eight Bells on Broadway—The Story O. Henry Never Wrote—When Ignorance is Golden—Where Good Yachtsmen Got Together—The Partridgers' Famous Party

Chapter 6   71
　The Contract with a Washout—Before the Boom—An Age of Sandwich Snatchers—Trained-Seal Etiquette

Chapter 7   81
　On Tipping—Hot Dogs—Cultured Commission Merchants—Under Royal Protection

Chapter 8   91
　An Ante-prohibition Bartender—Dainty Morsels at Secondhand—And When the Pie was Opened—The Barber-shop Blues—A Fashionable Ringside—Fights Staged at Rector's

Chapter 9   105
　Good Linen Dies Young—The Lonesomest Day in the Year—Steak à la Fifteen Minutes—A Giant Bouquet of Greens—The Chef's Favourite Perfume

Chapter 10   117
　A Check on the Bad News—The Original Yes Man—That Apple-Sauce Joke—A Profitable Side Line—A Pocketful of Marbles—Mistakes Will Happen

Chapter 11 — 129

The Great Sport of Eating—A Lamb in Boarding-House Clothing—When West Meets East—Jewels from Russia—To be Served on Blotters—Economical Extravagance—A Good System Gone Wrong—The Horsey Dinner—Lone-Wolf Eccentricities—A Water-Marked Check

Chapter 12 — 149

Home Cooking—Origin of the Cover Charge—Luke's Guest of Honour—A Great Little Guy—Lackaye's Definition of Tact—Ringing a Dumb-Bell

Chapter 13 — 161

Old-Time Snicks and Snacks—The High Cost of Free Lunches—The Big Train in Politics—Just Between Friends—Sacred to the Memory

Chapter 14 — 173

Lots in a Name—More Noise than Nourishment—Terpsichorean Teams—To the Stage via Rector's

Chapter 15 — 183

Then Came the War—Cake Eaters and Lounge Lizards—Ling Rector Foo's Place—A Popular Road House—To Insure Poor Service—Food and Fist Fights—Bad News for Business Men—Pleasant Memories

Chapter 1

The Man Who Changed Broadway

For a lady who never existed, the Girl from Rector's was very real. She was the creation of Paul Potter, the playwright, who was struggling with the translation of a French farce for Al Woods. Paul had progressed nicely in the work with the exception that the piece lacked an appropriate American title. I do not remember the exact date, but it was just about the high-bicycle age, when two bags of laundry and a Babylonian garden on the horizon would later prove to be a lady with leg-o'-mutton sleeves under a picture hat. That is what the well-dressed woman thought that dressing well was. If the time is still hazy in your mind, I will enlighten you with the information that rubber plants were still legal within the city limits and pug dogs snapped at book agents with almost human intuition.

Like all the other writers of that day who had problems to figure out, Paul turned his steps toward Rector's, meanwhile mulling the title over in his mind. A slight drizzle set in, and as he reached our restaurant a hansom cab drove up and a very pretty girl stepped out. Her skirts were raised a trifle higher than schoolgirls wore them then and a trifle lower than grandmothers wear them now. She made a beautiful picture, and in a flash the observant Potter had his title for his farce. It was *The Girl from Rector's*.

Ah, she was piquant, petite and fair to gaze upon, was the Girl from Rector's. She raised our establishment to the highest peak of prosperity and popularity. But like all fickle prima donnas, her smile spelled ruination, and she was to tumble us into the dust at the end. Even before the advent of prohibition and its chain of padlocked stores across the nation, the doom of Rector's was sealed, betrayed by the Girl from Rector's. How did she do it?

Well, my father and myself had made a million in our restaurant business and had built a magnificent hotel, also named Rector's. Both of our projects were going along very nicely until the Girl stepped out of the cab in the rain. For *The Girl from Rector's* was the first of the naughty Parisian plays and she acquired nationwide fame; so much so that when an out-of-town buyer wrote home to his wife on Hotel Rector stationery, no sooner was that loving epistle opened and the contents duly noted than the long-distance telephone wires grew heliotrope with congested wifely indignation and Mr. Out-of-Town-Buyer got marital instruction to move lock, stock, and barrel out of that terrible hotel where the Girl from Rector's made her habitat. The result was a crash which carried the restaurant with it when we were unable to meet our notes; and I vividly remember my father, in another rainstorm, standing in front of a poster on which the Girl from Rector's was smiling capriciously. She held a glass of champagne and seemed to beckon to us as drops of moisture, which may have been rain, trickled down my father's cheeks. The Girl had a short life, but she saw many things. Rector's may not have been the center of population in the late '90s and the early 1900s, but it was the center of all the population worth knowing. Still, if you are not to blame it all on Broadway, then I am frankly unable to blame it all on the Girl. I, myself, must shoulder the majority of the blame. For I am the man who changed Broadway.

The man who changed Broadway. Whether this be a citation or an indictment, nevertheless it is so. I found Broadway a quiet little lane of ham and eggs in 1899, and I left it a full-blown avenue of lobsters, champagne, and morning-afters. I brought Paris to New York and improved it by the transplanting. When Broadway grew jaded and lost its appetite I pampered it with the provender of the gods, simmering in the sauces of Olympus. When Broadway sat down to eat I prodded it to its feet with irresistible music. And when Broadway sought to sleep I turned day into night and night into daze.

For almost a quarter of a century Rector's was the supreme court of triviality, where who's who went to learn what's what. It was the cathedral of froth, where New York chased the rainbow, and the butterfly netted the entomologist. It was the national museum of habits, the bourse of gossip, and the clearing house of rumors. No personal triumph was complete unless validated by an evening at Rector's, in much the same way that the conqueror exhibited the conquered in a procession through the arches of ancient and imperial Rome.

Please Step into My Parlor

Champions, challengers, opera stars, explorers, captains of industry and lieutenants of sloth; gamblers, authors, and adventurers—all celebrated their temporary successes with a night at Rector's, and I know that Broadway did not really believe that Peary had discovered the Pole or Dewey defeated the Spanish fleet until it saw them both in my restaurant. My clientèle numbered the best and the greatest in the land, and was the incubator which hatched that man without a country, the head waiter.

But what an institution! There, hidden behind the palms and listening to the strains of a Russian symphony, one could forget—and two could be forgotten.

When I say that I am the man who changed Broadway, I am challenging a street many miles long. I changed only a section of it, known as the Roaring Forties, located between the Aspirin Belt and the Petrified Forest of Lampposts. But I certainly changed that section where the electric-light sign rises at twilight and sets at dawn. And there must be many an aged sufferer from gout and kindred accomplishments of old age whose expert chauffeuring of a wheel chair in crowded traffic is due to the kindly hand and menu of Rector's.

Wining and dining in the old days was more or less a major operation. And it was Rector's that introduced dancing with meals. If you hate lobster do not point the finger of anger at the ocean, for I must also balance that blame on my devoted head. I introduced the hard-boiled crustacean to the avenue of tinsel. If somewhere in your prewar memory there is a throbbing recollection of champagne and lobster fighting the internal struggle of indigestion, once again it was Rector's that blazed the way on the tungsten frontier when the wine agent roved the prairies in countless herds.

I take no great pride in my achievements. Lobster, champagne, and supper dances are surely the trinity of uselessness. The champagne has gone long since, even though the labels will not down. The lobster and the supper dances still remain, much to the annoyance of the average individual who can eat a lobster but doesn't relish it as a partner in a dance. But I do take exceptional pride in the fact that Rector's was the center of the web spun by the benevolent spider of Manhattan in its efforts to snare the genius and ability of America.

Truly, New York is hated by some in much the same way that London must be hated by the rest of England, and Paris envied by rural France. For these capitals drain their native lands of the artist, the singer, and the writer, who all must come to dispose of their unique wares. And I catered to them all for many years.

When the wick of reminiscence is burning brightly in the oil of memory, I see O. Henry, Stephen Crane, Lillian Russell, the Whitneys, Oscar Hammerstein, Rex Beach, Montgomery and Stone, Eugene Field, Paul Armstrong, Tad, Diamond Jim Brady, David Graham Phillips, Stanford White—it seems that I see Stanford White again as he sat that last evening in Rector's, enjoying life to the fullest, unaware that the upper half of the hourglass contained but a few sands of life. It was a Wednesday evening and the finish was to come in a few days, but in a different establishment, thank heaven. But even had White known, I do not think it would have made any difference to him, as he was a peculiar compound of genius and iconoclast who asked nothing of the finger of Fate except that it be well manicured. Had the event occurred in Rector's, then it would have been the first and only scandal in the history of a family of caterers whose business life dated back to 1825.

Change Partners

True, the Girl from Rector's was not a Quaker maiden, and very often divorcee bowed to divorcee and wondered who was the new sultan's favorite. I once had the unique honor of escorting three married couples to the same table, and, believe it or not, every one of the three men had been married at one time in his career to every one of the three ladies in the party! They spent a pleasant evening together, although I imagine family histories were not the topic of the conversation. Yet there were no battles in my place, although there was no doubt that many of the diners brought along their war maps to lay out future campaigns and skirmishes.

It was very difficult to keep track of the different couples from year to year, as appendicitis and divorces were just becoming popular, in the order named. The romances withered, flourished, and withered again, just as romances do to-day. It was extremely foolish to try to keep tabs on a man like Nat Goodwin, as he himself was never sure which one of the beautiful ladies dining and dancing was his present wife.

I think the situation was described best by Wilson Mizner after spending several years in the Klondike during the gold rush. He was a wit whose bons mots could not always be published and whose biting sarcasm made Voltaire's bitterest efforts feeble by contrast. When Mizner landed back in New York his first visit, of course, was to Rector's to greet his old friends. It was just the shank of the evening when Wilson arrived, and I greeted him warmly. The place was crowded with the beauty and chivalry of New York. He stood at the entrance, surveying the crowded room, his gaze flitting from couple to couple.

Then he said, "The same old faces. But they're paired off differently."

But to return to Stanford White. He was a great first-nighter, and on that Wednesday evening had enjoyed his first show since his return from France. He was dressed immaculately, as usual, and was alone, which was unusual. I instructed the head waiter to place Mr. White at a small single table facing the door. Somehow the only thing I remember very distinctly about his evening dress is that he was wearing patent-leather shoes. So was I and so were all the waiters.

A young man entered hurriedly. He also was wearing patent-leather shoes. He gazed around in a wild manner that was noticeable. I assisted him with his light spring overcoat and caused the tails of his evening dress coat to catch on an object in his hip pocket. The object was a revolver. The young man, a scion of a wealthy Pittsburgh family, looked jerkily around the room until his glance fell on White, who returned his stare in an unconcerned manner. The young fellow turned very pale, made a motion toward his hip, hesitated, and then turned and fled. Whatever he intended doing, he had lost his nerve.

He was to regain it sufficiently in a few days to place that gun against White's ear and pull the trigger.

But that is tragedy, and easily forgotten when basking in the reflected glory of one of Berry Wall's new cravats. Berry was one of our most insistent patrons, and rarely an evening passed that he didn't drop in to pass the time of night—and then forget it. He was the best-dressed man in all America and Europe. I never heard of anybody disputing his title, so I imagine that the other great continents were his by default. His waistcoats, cravats, and braided coats were the envy and despair of Fifth Avenue. I cannot describe the glory of his raiment, but I think Joseph's brothers threw Joseph down the well for less provocation. Some idea of Berry's grandeur in haberdashery may be gleaned by Marshall P. Wilder's solemn statement that Berry had raglan shoulders in his pajamas and wore lapels on his underwear.

Painting the Lily

Wilton Lackaye, one of our greatest actors, observed Berry promenading into Rector's one evening and blinked at the superb assemblage of good taste. Berry was wearing a pearl derby, white vest, cutaway coat, and had a flower in his buttonhole. Wilton stared a minute and then said, in the dry manner that would make the Sahara Desert almost a lush meadow, "Add spats and stir with a cane." Lackaye is a wit who is not properly appreciated in America, which may be due to his refusal to resort to the vernacular. His command of English is so perfect that his victims often wonder what the crowd is laughing about. Wilton is the man who, having lost one of a valuable pair of cuff links in his club, hung up the remaining link on the club bulletin board over this notice: "Lost—The mate to this cuff link. Will buy or sell."

When you had Wilton Lackaye, William Collier, George Cohan, and Rennold Wolf all seated in a foursome in your restaurant, then you were a very happy host indeed, because here were four of the greatest wits the world ever knew. Money could not buy a reservation in Rector's at any time if a regular patron first put in a bid for the table. It was only recently at an Army and Navy Club dinner that Collier arose to speak after a dreary hour's lecture by an admiral, followed by an equally gloomy hour's eulogy by a general. Collier's entire speech was: "Ladies or gentlemen, now I know what they mean by the Army and Navy forever."

Just a trifle longer than the famous speech delivered by the same Lackaye at a Tuesday-afternoon meeting of an amateur dramatic society. They had been trying to snare Lackaye for years, but he dreaded amateur theatricals. Finally, after many letters and many telephone calls, he consented to speak, provided that the meeting would not be of more than twenty or thirty minutes' duration. But when he actually showed up in person the chairman of the society was delighted and proceeded to paint the glories of Lackaye in all the colors of an oratorical rainbow clashing with the splendor of a Websterian aurora borealis. The speech went on, while the unfortunate Lackaye fidgeted in his chair. Finally, after two hours, when the chairman felt that the subject had been well done on both sides, he turned to Wilton and with a flourish said, "The guest of honor will now give us his address."

The guest of honor arose and said, "My address is the Lambs Club." And it was.

Chapter 2

Dan Daly's Escargots

The remarkable thing about the famous actors and writers of the good old nights—I almost wrote "good old days"—was that with few exceptions no particular dish seems to have been their favorite. That is, they all had well-balanced appetites, were in good health, and could enjoy any food their fancy dictated. Of course there were exceptions, and one of these was Dan Daly, who starred with Edna May in *The Belle of New York*. Twenty-five years ago we had not yet arrived at that bugaboo of the gourmet—the scientific diet.

Just as good wine needs no bush, we figured that good food required no explanation. Therefore I do not know the amount of vitamins concealed within the neat but compact body of an adult snail. There may be plenty and there may be few. But there must be some, for Daly lived on snails for two years! It must have been through some queer quirk of his palate, because he seemed normal and vigorous enough at all times.

He performed on the stage during those two years, and did well. Yet I know that he ate nothing but snails because he never ate at all during the day and ate but one meal after midnight.

That one meal was in Rector's. He was his own dietitian. He had been a moderate eater and drinker for many years, until he suddenly went on a snail formula and followed it for twenty-four months. Then he passed quietly away, as befitting his singular diet, but not until he had accounted for many thousand snails. Although it may be a little late to mention it now, Mr. Daly always washed the snails gently down with two pints of champagne.

Mr. Daly drank none but the best wine and ate none but the finest imported snails. The domestic animal, or insect, is a hustling individual whose vigorous life in the wide open spaces unfits it for table use in the better class of hostelries. Mr. Daly's snails were the escargots à la Burgundy, the snail of Burgundy, raised from pups in the South of France under the most refining of influences. It comes from the certified escargot stock, for even snails have ancestry in La Belle France. Warmed by the Riviera sunshine and fanned by the Mediterranean breezes, it pursues the even tenor of its way, never hurrying, never getting excited. It feeds on the leaf of the Burgundian grape, from which vine is derived the finest of vintages. Which is why our American snail has been driven off the market. It requires a lifetime of training even to be a snail. Escargots à la Burgundy! All other snails are impostors. It was a splendid diet, and Mr. Daly's demise proved nothing to the contrary. It may have been the champagne. I never tasted a snail myself.

He was the only regular snail connoisseur we had, although some tourists and morbid bystanders would occasionally order a few, just to write home to the folks about it. I might add that we did everything to make the snails happy in their adopted home. Each snail was accompanied by its pedigree, and whenever possible our European agent forwarded its pet name to us under separate cover. We did everything to make our snails happy, even to shipping them in individual barrels, each barrel stuffed with the fresh leaves of Burgundian grapevine. In spite of all our efforts, our snail trade was limited strictly to the diner whose French vocabulary consisted of a doubtful finger pointed at an equally doubtful word in French. So the entire consumption of snails was confined to those unfortunates who had pointed with pride to escargots à la Burgundy and were compelled by the same pride to go through with it.

Another and more famous eater, but for different reasons, was Diamond Jim Brady. I can affirm and testify, after looking over the books of that dim era, that Diamond Jim was the best twenty-five customers we had!

You will probably recall him as the man who offered Hopkins—I mean the college and not the actress—one hundred thousand dollars in gold if the Hopkins surgeons could give him a new stomach—one from an elephant preferred. The Johns Hopkins surgeons could not perform the feat, but I understand that Diamond Jim left the hospital a magnificent sum for prolonging his life several years.

Diamond Jim's Lighting System

He was an odd character, and the first of the successful salesmen who utilized the bright lights of Broadway to promote the sale of his commodities. His name was derived from his jewelry, and when Diamond Jim had all his illumination in place, he looked like an excursion steamer at twilight. He had powerful diamonds in his shirt front that cast beams strong enough to sunburn an unwary pedestrian. He had diamonds in his cuffs and actually wore diamond suspender buttons, fore and aft. The fore may have been good taste, but the aft were parvenu. He wore diamonds on his fingers and there was a rumor that he had diamond bridge work. His vest buttons also were precious stones, and I think that when remonstrated with for his excessive display of gems, Mr. Brady remarked, "Them as has 'em wears 'em."

Although his business life led him among the bright lights, Diamond Jim never smoked or drank. But how he ate! He loved to be surrounded by handsome men and beautiful women at the table, and it was no unusual thing for us to lay covers for eight or ten guests of Mr. Brady. If they all kept their appointments, fine! If but two or three were able to be present, fine! And if nobody showed up but Diamond Jim, fine! Mr. Brady proceeded gravely to eat the ten dinners himself.

It is possible to obtain some idea of his terrific capacity by his average menu under normal conditions. When I say he never drank, I mean intoxicating beverages. His favorite drink was orange juice. I knew just what he wanted, and before he appeared at the table I always commandeered the most enormous carafe in the house. This was filled to the brim with orange juice and cracked ice. He tossed that off without quivering a chin. It was immediately replaced with a duplicate carafe, to be followed by a third, and possibly a fourth before the dinner was over and the last waiter had fainted in the arms of an exhausted chef.

The next item was oysters. Mr. Brady was very fond of sea food. He would eat two or three dozen Lynnhaven oysters, each measuring six inches from tip to tail, if an oyster has either. Wilson Mizner, observing Diamond Jim eating oysters, remarked, "Jim likes his oysters sprinkled with clams." Observing the same diner from a near-by listening post, Mr. Mizner also continued his observations with "Jim likes his sirloin steaks smothered in veal cutlets."

After Diamond Jim had nibbled daintily on three dozen papa oysters, it would be an even bet that he would order another dozen or so just to relieve the monotony. Then would follow a dozen hard-shell crabs, claws and all. There was no soup, which discounts Mizner's statement that Jim fanned the soup with his hat.

Diamond Jim was a gentleman, even though he did wear his napkin around his neck. But this was not due to lack of etiquette, but rather to the conformation of Mr. Brady's topography. A napkin on his knee would have been as inadequate as a doily under a bass drum. Diamond Jim's stomach started at his neck and swelled out in majestic proportions, gaining power and curve as it proceeded southward. Therefore the only place where a napkin would have done him any good was around his neck. And there he wore it. It looked like a bookmark in a tome of chins.

An Earnest Eater

After the crabs, then would come the deluge of lobsters. Lobsters were Rector's specialty and I took special pride in serving none but the finest. Six or seven giants would suffice. Diamond Jim ate them like an expert and cracked their claws like a man. There was no waste except the actual bony structure, which was dropped gracefully aside. A bus boy removed the debris as rapidly as it accumulated, otherwise Diamond Jim would have been in the same fix as the American gunboat in China.

This is a story told me by Doctor Kaveney, now a surgeon on the flagship of the Pacific fleet, but then an interne at Bellevue. He relates that after the Civil War, two side-paddle gunboats, originally destined for the conflict but finished too late, were detailed for duty in the Orient. The first was anchored outside Hong-Kong for a year. During that year all the sailors ate was beef. They dined on beef broth, beef stew, roast beef, and beef croquettes. The beef bones were discarded over the side. At the end of the year the first gunboat was ordered home and the second side paddler moved in to take her place. Kaveney swears that the second gunboat ran aground on the beef bones and was lost with all on board. In corroboration of his story, he says that to this day the reef is known as Beef Bone Ledge.

Anyway, we removed all the victims of Jim's dinner as fast as we could bring up the ambulances. Then he would order a steak and toy with it until it vanished. But steaks and chops were not his hobby. He loved sea food. Coffee, cakes, and pastry would follow. He selected his cakes carefully—in handfuls. When he pointed at a platter of French pastry he didn't mean any special piece of pastry. He meant the platter.

Then he would order a two-pound box of bonbons from the candy girl and pass them around among his guests. If any guest took a piece of the candy Diamond Jim would then order another two-pound box for himself. In fact, so great was his love of sweets that he bought a controlling interest in the biggest of candy factories of that time.

He tipped very liberally, because he loved life and wanted everybody to enjoy life with him. I never saw the man do an unkind thing during all the years I knew him. There is no exaggeration in the details of his dinner, because I served him many and he relished every one. He was more of a gourmet than a gourmand, if you can perceive the line of demarcation between the two. If there is any reader who thinks that I am taking a ghoulish delight in rehashing the account of Diamond Jim Brady's personal habits, all I can say is that I wish I could have enjoyed Rector's cuisine as Diamond Jim did. Furthermore, he was a man who spent his money lavishly. Anybody could get a thousand from him in the days when a thousand dollars was an incredible sum. If you don't think it was, just hark back to the diaries of Rockefeller and Ford and read their stories of how they saved their first thousand. To-day a thousand is nothing.

His friends used to remonstrate with him and caution him against the many leeches who preyed on him. Even I, although merely a servant seeking to please my patrons, took advantage of our friendship and said, "Mr. Brady, you shouldn't encourage these people. They haven't the slightest intention of paying you back. They are trimming you."

Mr. Brady said, "H'm"—he was munching candy—"what do you mean?"

I replied, "Just what I said. They are making a sucker out of you."

He answered me with the retort that proved the business acumen that lay under that massive frame. His rejoinder was a thorough analysis of his entire character, which was a desire to be a free spender and at the same time know what he was accomplishing with his money. He had no illusions about the butterflies who hovered around the gleaming torches in his shirt front. He knew them far better than they knew him, because every night he wasted with them was not a night wasted for him. He piled up millions while spending thousands.

What he answered was: "Being a sucker is fun—if you can afford it."

It is a classic. It is a good thing to remember. And he was right. Remember that remark. It applies equally well to the collector of antique furniture, ancient paintings, or investors in the relative speeds of horses and the pulling power of strong-armed jockeys. It's fun if you can afford it.

I almost forgot to add that when Diamond Jim had dinner in Rector's it was the usual prelude to an evening at the theatre. On the way to the show he would stop his cab at a store and purchase another two-pound box of candy manufactured by the company he controlled. That would be finished before the curtain rose, and it was nothing unusual for him to buy another box between acts. After the show he would return to Rector's for a midnight snack.

Oysters in Tin Shells

He was an unusual personage, but then we dealt in unusual personages at Rector's. And of all the odd characters, I think there was not one more commanding and unusual than my own father, the founder of Rector's in Chicago and New York. He was a remarkable man.

And here I have a confession to make. In spite of the foreign atmosphere and elaborate French menu, the Rector family was intensely American. My grandfather founded the famous Frontier House at Lewiston, on the Niagara River, in 1825. Here, under the sign of the griffin, which was to be our family trade-mark almost a century later on Broadway, he served the French, English, American, and Indian woodsmen and trappers. Then he moved to Lockport on the Erie Canal, and it was in this little town that my father was born in the second Rector hotel.

When the Civil War began, Father enlisted in the Ninth Heavy Artillery, New York. His older brother was a captain in the same company and was killed at Fredericksburg. Father and Grandfather called on President Lincoln in Washington and received his personal permission to have Captain Rector's body removed from the Fredericksburg cemetery to New York State.

A few years after the war Father married Louise Petersen, daughter of William Petersen, in whose home on Tenth Street Lincoln breathed his last. The young couple came to New York, where Father became a conductor on the Second Avenue surface line, running through the famous Bowery.

A few years later he was in charge of the first Pullman hotel dining car that ever ran across the continent. A man who could step from horse cars to Pullmans would naturally have no timidity about opening up a dining room in Chicago. Which was just what Father did, in the basement on the southeast corner of Clark and Monroe streets, where the Rector Building stands today.

He decided to specialize in sea food, and ancient Chicagoans remember him as the man who parlayed a fifteen-cent oyster stew into a million dollars. At that time all fish and oysters, travelling west to see America first, were controlled by the Booth Fisheries. Father determined to make an experiment, as he was tired of getting his oysters in hermetically sealed cans. No Chicagoan had ever seen an oyster reposing in state on its own mother-of-pearl throne. So we arranged for the first barrel of oysters ever to be shipped West in their own shells.

The experiment was a success. We tried it with the Rockaway oyster, and I still remember the day they arrived and we knocked the lid off the barrel in fear and trembling. A trial oyster was quickly opened and proved to be in full command of its faculties after thirty hours' journey. The barrel lasted about ten minutes.

George Ade, Sam Bernard, and Elbert Hubbard were among the vanguard of loyal Chicagoans who rushed into Rector's and defeated the invading bivalve. After that, any oyster entering Chicago did so under its own cover. We next showed the amazed citizens of Illinois their first live lobster, and then topped that with the first live green sea turtle from the West Indies. It weighed three hundred pounds in its stocking feet. It celebrated its debut in the Middle West by knocking over a lamp in the freight depot and setting the building on fire. The blaze didn't reach the magnificent proportions of the conflagration sponsored by the left hind foot of Mrs. O'Leary's cow, but it was not so bad for a turtle's first effort.

Tea Time at the World's Fair

But that turtle had sung its terrapin song, for once again Chicago mustered its reserves and attacked the maritime expeditionary force. Mr. Turtle lasted about three days in the form of turtle chowder, soup, and steaks. Chicago ate and talked turtle for three days, and some disappointed customers appeased their unrequited affection for turtle meat by carving their initials in the shell. However, enough oysters and terrapin arrived in the next ten years to satisfy all. It started as a fad, but is now a necessity to Illinois health, owing to the fact that the rivers of the Middle West are draining the soil of iodine, and iodine is strongly predominant in all sea food.

Chicagoans must have been grateful to the Rectors, for we obtained the privilege of operating the only restaurant inside the World's Fair grounds in 1893. It was the Café Marine, and its specialties, of course, were the treasures gleaned from the fishing banks.

Would it be betraying an old secret to say that the ladies visiting the Café Marine seemed to be very fond of afternoon tea? I doubt that Sir Thomas Lipton ever grew this tea on his plantations in the Far East. And although the teacups were beautiful Chinese porcelain the contents had a Scotch aroma which was more thistles than heather. After two or three cups of this tea, I have seen the ladies walk away, clinging to their flimsy parasols like parachute jumpers to the cross bars of their trapezes. It may have been tea, or it may not, but it was in teacups. You can settle the question for yourself by remembering that kittens born in an oven are not necessarily biscuits.

A Restaurant Gridiron

It was also in the Café Marine that the first lady smoked the first cigarette in public. It created a furor among the monitors of late-Victorian morals, but as the lady happened to be Princess Eulalie, of Spain, the Chicago flappers of that decade immediately followed the fashion. The princess smoked in her own home, and she doubtless felt at home anywhere. I do not remember seeing the princess dabbling at one of our demi-tasse teacups, but she often ordered soup in a very deep dish.

The growing fame of the Chicago Rector's attracted every prominent man or woman who ever visited Chicago. We had also introduced vintage wines with fine results for us, if not for our customers. This brought us into contact with George Kessler. He told Father that the Rectors should move to New York, as we had become known through the word-of-mouth advertising spread by our friends in the theatrical profession. He had the spot on Broadway picked out in advance. It was a building designed for a restaurant, built by Charles T. Barney, president of the Knickerbocker Trust Company, and leased to Jack Dunston and Thomas Healy, both of whom were to become well-known Bonifaces in later years. The deal had fallen through owing to some dissension. Dunston opened the historic Jack's restaurant, only recently closed. Year after year, athletic victories of all kinds were celebrated in Jack's. Year after year, Yale, Harvard, and Princeton struggled for the football championship only to have the victorious team defeated on the night of victory by the renowned Jack's flying wedge of waiters. Healy opened his own place also, only to succumb to the modern kitchenette and the keener competition of homebrewing.

Bert Shaw, of Chicago, who organized the National Biscuit Company, and was the man who put the first custom-made soda cracker on the market, joined with Kessler in urging us to go to New York. We went. The New York Rector's was opened on September 23, 1899. About a week later Manhattan Island was celebrating Dewey's return from Manila. We were told that our Chicago reputation had preceded us, but there was no way of advertising in those days, although we had plenty of notices in theatrical trade papers.

Although the building had been erected by Barney as a restaurant property, we had an advance expense of more than two hundred thousand dollars—nearly a quarter of a million dollars invested in hypothetical goodwill. We opened our doors on a fine day in late September, not knowing whether anybody was going to come in or not.

While I am speaking of firsts, I may as well boast that the Rector front door was the first revolving door in New York. We sat back and wondered whether it would revolve. It did. It spun madly and Father and I bowed and scraped our first welcome to our first New York patron. But nobody entered, although the revolving door continued to whirl like a mechanical dervish.

We investigated, and discovered that the delighted youth of Manhattan was throwing itself into the revolving door just for the trip. All that afternoon the curious crowds continued to pack the compartments of Rector's revolving door. At least five thousand people pivoted around and around in a joyful, if belated, Maypole dance. Some folks even went home to bring their relatives down to enjoy the free journey, while Rector père, and Rector fils, dealers in marine food, gazed upon the queer fish trapped in their spinning aquarium.

Another Round-Tripper

Twilight of the same afternoon seemed to have arrived a year later as a solitary horse cab stopped in front of our place and a figure in formal evening dress stepped out. It was a fine-looking elderly gentleman who alighted and dismissed the cabby with a tip. As the leader of our Russian symphony orchestra stood with baton poised to give the signal that was to launch the musicians on their career, and fifty waiters stood on tiptoe ready to pounce on the first patron, the elderly gentleman gingerly entered the revolving door. He took a deep breath as if expecting the air to give out before he completed the trip. We stood by, taking much deeper breaths, as we did not know whether he would prove real or whether he was only another excursionist. The door swung halfway. Would he come in or would he complete the round trip? He came in, the music struck up, and Father took his coat while I grabbed his hat. He sat down and ordered—an Italian dinner!

We bowed him out gracefully. The music stopped automatically, the waiters relaxed, and Father turned to me and said, "I'd like some spaghetti myself."

Then the door whirled again, but not so quickly as the two Rectors.

Chapter 3

EVAPORATION OF SILVERWARE

The first man actually to come through our famous revolving door was George Kessler, the man who had advised us to come on from Chicago. We did not know whether we were glad to see him. We feared that he had some more advice. My father had left Chicago known as the man who had run an oyster stew into a million. But right at this moment it looked as if we would run the million back into the stew.

Kessler was astounded at the beauty of the place. There were 100 tables downstairs and 75 tables on the second floor, exclusive of the four private dining rooms which were later to be the scene of many famous dinners given by Reginald Vanderbilt, Alfred Gwynne Vanderbilt, Freddy Gebhard, John Jacob Astor, Jesse Lewisohn, Sarah Bernhardt, Mrs. Leslie Carter, Harry Lehr, Lillian Russell, David Belasco, Charles Frohman, Larry Waterbury, Joseph Jefferson, and Sir Henry Irving.

The walls of the main dining room were lined with mirrors reaching to the ceiling. The decorations, in green and gold, were of the period of Louis XIV, whose main idea in life must have been to overshadow the glories of the other Louis'. The table linen was imported from Belfast, with the famous Rector griffin interwoven in the fabric. The silverware was made to order by the most famous of American silversmiths. In spite of the fact that it was stenciled with the Rector griffin, it became very popular among our patrons. Our loss among souvenir hunters was about 2,000 pieces of silverware a year, including demi-tasse spoons, bouillon spoons, sugar tongs, graduating in size up to a coffee percolator. In figuring wear and tear by the year, we always allowed $20,000 for evaporation in silverware. This is a conservative estimate.

If a patron asked for a spoon or a knife as a memento of a pleasant evening, we gladly gave it to him, and also made him a present of an imported ash tray bearing a picture showing the exterior of our place.

But if we detected a customer stuffing tableware into his or her pockets like a travelling man packing a trunkful of samples, we added the cost of the articles to the dinner check.

A Hot Time in the Old Town

The highest figure we ever assessed any dinner party for violation of the ethics of hospitality was exactly seventy-eight dollars. The check was not disputed. Even though there was no explanatory item with the additional seventy-eight dollars, the host paid it willingly, although the entire check amounted to only ninety-one dollars. At that, I think he made a good bargain, as his party, when walking out, sounded like Kriss Kringle's reindeer in full jingle on a frosty night. This was one time when the clink of my outgoing silverware was music to my ears. The host proved that evening that the greatest after-dinner speech ever made was "Bring me the check."

I think the climax in souvenir collecting was reached one pleasant evening in winter when a lady carried out an eight-pound coffee percolator under her ermine evening wrap. The wrap was worth about $8,000. The percolator cost about $75. Broadway was amazed that evening by seeing a lady and gentleman leap out of a blazing two-wheeler hansom cab. The lady had forgotten to extinguish the motive power of the percolator, which was alcohol. I think the lady was using the same motive power. The cabman sued her for a blistered hansom cab and a scorched horse. We got the percolator back, but it was melted down to a thimble. The lady lost $7,025 by the transaction. She was half cooked when she took the percolator, but was fortunate that she didn't finish well broiled. Her ermine coat was done to a crisp.

Hansom cabs were very popular in those days as a means of locomotion. You could hire them around three dollars an hour or strike a bargain by haggling with the cabby over the rate per trip. It was cheaper by the hour. The old hansom cab possessed a romance not associated with the modern taxicab. In the first place, the driver of the hansom was on top the cab and his horse wore blinkers. Two sweethearts could spoon in the cab even though their chaperon was following them on a bicycle.

The modern taxi is different, and a kiss in one is somewhat similar to an embrace in a show window. Good soldiers never look back. Neither do good chauffeurs. Still, though you could put blinkers on the horse, you cannot put them on a driver. I still chuckle over Nat Wills' story of being driven with his girl over to Brooklyn. The chauffeur stopped his car in the middle of the bridge.

Nat ordered the driver to continue, but he retorted, "The girl hollered 'Stop!'"

The girl said, "I wasn't talking to you."

Ali Rabit's Luxury

Outside of the hansom cab that was eliminated in the tournament with the blazing percolator, the cab which suffered the most was the one that tried to wrestle with

Ham Fish. Ham, whose full name was Hamilton Fish, was credited with having picked up a complete hansom cab, equipped with one horse, pedigree unknown, one dozing driver, and a broken whip, and turning the whole outfit completely over with its sunny side up like an egg on a skillet. He was very powerful.

I did not see this feat of strength, as the name of Ham Fish is emblazoned forever on the golden scroll of those who died at Guantanamo in '98.

Everybody travelled in hansom cabs in those days. John Kendrick Bangs was the hero of probably the only parade of these peculiar vehicles ever held. He left Rector's one morning, when this twentieth century was still new, in a cab and was jaunting along merrily when he spied an ordinary cat belonging to the genus known as alley rabbit. John was possessed of a very warm heart and he ordered his cabby to stop while he petted the hungry and gaunt junior feline. It was as scrawny and as mangy as its more famous brother which Brian G. Hughes was to enter in an aristocratic show of Maltese and Persian mousers. It failed to win first prize only because it meowed an octave too low. This was a mild prank by Hughes, who was the greatest practical joker in history. He won a blue ribbon in a Madison Square Garden Show with a noble horse whose name was Puldekar Orphan.

Puldekar Orphan was easily the finest stepper in the show, but Brian had his blue ribbon well exhibited about town before the judges deciphered Puldekar Orphan and discovered that it meant "pulled a car often."

Hughes had picked up the cat and the horse at the same auction. The horse, true to his name, had often pulled a crosstown car, and not always willingly. Hughes took both the horse and the cat, fattened them up and made blue ribbons the laughing-stock of the town.

Bangs's cat was not destined for a show, but it did figure in the parade. A salty tear dribbled down Bangs's cheek as he stroked the rough fur of the ill-fed fence wolf. He decided to adopt it and give it a good home. But the cabby objected to the presence of such a creature in his freshly upholstered hansom. An argument which followed, and in which the cat took no part, was stopped by the fortunate appearance of a second hansom, whose driver was about to take sides with his brother charioteer until he learned that Bangs was anxious to hire his vehicle for the accommodation of a distinguished foreigner, said foreigner being the cat.

Fare per mile was fixed without the aid of the Interstate Commerce Commission, and the cat became the sole occupant of the second hansom. The journey was resumed with Bangs in the lead, and the cat, stroking his whiskers, in second place. They proceeded merrily past monuments, parks, and important buildings. The betting at this stage was Bangs to win and the cat for the runner-up.

My, 'Twas a Hansom Parade!

Bangs was rolling along easily, musing on man's ingratitude to man, and especially to cats, when he suddenly thought that his new friend might be hungry. So he ordered a stop at an all-night delicatessen store, and going inside, purchased one adult herring. His first step outside the store was greeted by a royal salute of twenty-one meows by the cat, which was hungry enough to have smelled a sardine in the Seven Seas, and furthermore to have named the sea. In fact, its intense eagerness to get at the herring caused Bangs to think that overeating was even more of a breach of cab etiquette than overstarving. He decided to feed the kitty when he got home and started to climb into his cab. He was stopped by his jehu, who objected to the presence of a herring in his tumbril, owing to its effect on future patronage.

This was a stumper, as it was impossible to trust the herring in the second cab with the cat, which might kill itself through its natural anxiety to catch up on many delayed meals for its nine thin lives.

Once again good fortune came to the rescue in the form of a third hansom, which rumbled up empty but not forlorn. Bangs requisitioned this seagoing hack after bargaining for the accommodation of one passenger, name unknown. The passenger turned out to be the herring, and with Bangs in the van, the three carts swung into the line of march, with the cat a good second and the herring a poor third.

That's the way they finished. Bangs first, the cat second, and the herring just nosing in for show money. A little later, I think the cat was entitled to both second and third places, as he was purring dreamily on Bangs's hearth with the added starter reposing in his stomach. It required three hansom cabs to give that cat a square meal in a roundabout way. I never found out whether kitty appreciated its foster guardian's interest in its welfare. But Bangs had the consolation of knowing that it was a herring well spent.

Like all philosophers, Bangs hated to see dumb animals suffer. He was a natural humorist and was probably the only man who ever rode under an arch of triumph with an escort consisting of a cat and a herring. This is one story which gets funnier with each repetition. I defy any man to think up a more laughable sequence of charitable foolishness than the one I have just related, which is positively true—at least, Bangs said it was true. It is his statement, and I stick to it.

But I started to tell you about the interior furnishings of Rector's and find myself drifting from the subject. Still,

I would rather speak of the people who patronized us than of the place itself. They were real, they were human, and they were lovable. The edifice itself means nothing without associations, and I think the finest line ever written is Edgar Guest's, "It takes a heap of living in a house to make it home." There was a heap of living in Rector's and it was heaped high.

As I said before, George Kessler was the first patron, but was followed closely by James J. Corbett and his wife. I was speaking to Mr. Corbett just the other day and he has always claimed to have been the first. But the honor, if any, belongs to Mr. Kessler.

Couple followed couple until our entire lower dining room was filled. There was no gradual budding of our establishment. Once we actually got started, we burst into full bloom.

The Divine Sarah in an Earthly Role

Can you imagine anybody being actually paid to drink champagne? But that was in the dim and dewy past. I almost said dim and dusty. The idea of the professional wine drinkers was to stimulate competition among the diners. And in wine drinking, just as in polo, golf, and yachting, the Simon-pure amateurs not only learned the sport but often defeated the professionals in fair and square competition.

The first onslaught on our kitchens almost overwhelmed us, but the harder our chefs breathed, the easier the Rectors exhaled and inhaled. We soon ran out of lobster and crab meat. Particularly the latter, because of the heavy demand for canapé of crab meat Rector.

This became a favorite dish of Sarah Bernhardt when that illustrious star toured this country. The divine Sarah would order one canapé after another, and would eat so much crab meat that we half expected her to scuttle sideways into the nearest pond. It might interest some readers to learn the recipe for the favorite dish of such a famous delineator of character roles. Here it is, exactly as served:

To half a pound of crab meat add a few cooked fresh mushrooms cut in slices, three tablespoonfuls of thick cream sauce, and season well. Place on a toasted hot muffin, spread with anchovy butter, and place over the top grated Parmesan cheese and bread crumbs. Bake and brown in a quick oven. Serve on a napkin and garnish with parsley.

It was really not quite so formidable as it sounds. The canapé citation meant anything that was served on toast or a muffin. It only had the wheel base of a sandwich. And that is what it was—an open-faced sandwich. The canapé was simply tacked onto the menu as the elephant was put in the riddle—just to make it more difficult.

I learned the recipe in Paris, where I had gone to observe the secret culinary rituals and savory machinations of the French chefs. I was detailed to this gastronomic espionage in much the same way that military men of a neutral nation are assigned as observers with the entangled armies of warring countries. Except that, in this case, I was an active participant in all the clashes of the pots and pans.

It came about in this manner: There was intense rivalry between ourselves, Delmonico's, and Sherry's. Mr. Louis Sherry went to his reward but recently. Although many of his patrons thought he was French, he was, like ourselves, intensely American, having been born in Vermont. With the wine, the music, and service being about equal in the three establishments, the rivalry naturally centered on the food. It was the ambition of each host to outdo his rivals in rare and toothsome viands. The tides of favor and patronage would fluctuate between the big three as each establishment flung a new and tantalizing aroma to the breezes, and noses would crinkle daintily in anticipation.

Diamond Jim Brady had been to Paris and brought home with him glad tidings of a famous dish—fillet of sole Marguery, prepared only in the Café de Marguery.

On the Trail of Sauce Marguery

At that time we were getting along famously, and I was studying law at Cornell University. Nevertheless, my father sent me to Paris in spite of the fact that I was in my third year at college and was preparing to graduate.

I never did get that diploma, but little dreamed of the honors which awaited me in Paris. I came to New York, consulted with Diamond Jim and my father, and received instructions, like the Spartan youth, to return either with the sauce Marguery or in it.

I still remember the jewels Diamond Jim was wearing that afternoon. He had been down to the track, and he wore the famous vest with diamond buttons, each button glittering like a harvest moon. His scarfpin was a horseshoe set with diamonds. When I say a horseshoe, I mean one for a race horse and not for a Shetland pony. Like a farmer weighing hay, Jim did things on a big scale.

His fingers were literally handcuffed with precious stones. When he pulled out his lead pencil I noted it particularly, for where ordinary pencils usually carried a rubber to erase mistakes, this prince of pencils carried a diamond the size of a nickel, but worth much more. The possessor of that diamond required no eraser for his mistakes.

His faithful bodyguard stood at his elbow, as always. He was a husky individual with an eternally tanned face—doubtless sunburned from continual exposure to Diamond Jim's jewels. We consulted all evening and I was appointed ambassador to the kitchens of Paris in order that Mr. Brady should again sop up the sauce Marguery. This is accomplished by holding a morsel of bread between the thumb and the index finger and sopping up the gravy. I think it is now called dunking in Greenwich Village, but there were no dunkers in our time. We lived in the sopping age.

Before going to Cornell, I had served two years in our own kitchens and was a qualified chef. I was in Paris in less than three weeks after Diamond Jim had evinced a desire for fillet of sole Marguery. It was with some trepidation that I presented my credentials at the Café de Paris, because I was to serve a belated apprenticeship in this restaurant. For, though the A.E.F. could say "Lafayette, we are here," I was forced to prove my ability before I could say I had arrived.

I worked for eight months as an apprentice cook in the kitchens of the Café de Paris. I learned the proper temperature of croutons, the correct humidity of consommé in an establishment where even knives and forks are laid out in true relation to the magnetic north and toothpicks have their latitude and longitude. Everything was figured out just so. The slightest swerve from ancestral routine was punished with reduction to the ranks.

But I was still far from sauce Marguery. There was another two months' sentence to serve as a bus boy to a venerable waiter who smoothed out a tablecloth as lovingly as an operating surgeon pats his apron. I learned to move silently and swiftly. Then came my promotion to a journeyman waitership with ceremonies befitting a coronation. But I had a good deal still to learn about a nation that has the culinary art drawn so fine it can detect the difference between the juice of the clam during times of political unrest and the same juice extracted from the clam at a period when the franc is at par. I had just served a regular patron sauce Bordelaise with cèpes, a dainty dish which this particular patron indulged in once every year, making an overland trip from Petrograd through a territory which, even then, was seething with dissension. He was a baron of old Russia with the finest beard I have ever seen hanging from a single chin. He was an epicure, but everything had gone along fine until this dish, which I was to bring over later and introduce to Rector's. As all the ingredients can be procured but one, I will tell you the secrets of sauce Bordelaise with cèpes Rector. We always added the word "Rector" to an imported dish:

> Chop fine two ounces of eschalots and place them in a saucepan with a lump of fresh butter and a little sweet oil. Allow to simmer for a few minutes. Add chopped cèpes and a glass of good claret. Allow it to reduce and add a pint of brown sauce.

All the necessary components of this delightful dish can be readily procured, except, of course, the glass of good claret. I know of no capable substitute. There was a benevolent look on my client's face as I served the dish, which was absolutely perfect and could only have been improved by the addition of a rainbow over the sauce. But one spoonful of the concoction and he exclaimed, "In the name of the sacred perfume! The curses of the Seven Orphans upon you! This is impossible!"

His taste was so fine that he had detected the fact that I had added the sweet oil before I had dropped in the fresh butter. I knew that he was right, but I had been careless and knew better than to argue with a patron. We were not so painstaking later on in America, where even the best of waiters might have lost patience and added the fresh butter to the baron's whiskers and distributed the sweet oil in the form of a shower bath. After this I was a bus boy for another thirty days.

It was as a bus boy that I think I saw the finest discrimination ever displayed by a diner. This gentleman was very finicky about his food and seemed to order for the pleasure of complaining. No one was just sure at what special moment this connoisseur of mistakes would break out in a tirade of shrill denunciation directed at the food, the service, or just general topics of the day. Everything had proceeded nicely in this instance and we were all hoping that he would break his own strict rule and leave in a good humor.

Prunes Wrong End To

Suddenly a plate crashed within an inch of my head and shattered to bits on the wall. A fleeing waiter dashed by me in a magnificent sprint which just enabled him to keep a pace ahead of a flying carafe. The gentle patron had suddenly gone berserk and was engaged in wrecking the place, while at the same time he was calling down the wrath of all the carved images of the South Seas on the waiter, the proprietor, and all his friends, even unto the third generation.

It was with great difficulty that a dozen of us managed to subdue him without retaliatory violence. A patron is always your guest—until he has paid his check. The head waiter sought to find out the trouble, but temporary *rigor mortis* had set in on the diner and his speech issued in the form of soap bubbles. We finally managed to get him seated in a chair, but he would not be satisfied until we sent for a gendarme. Meanwhile, the offending waiter was in hiding in the linen closet. Whatever his crime, the patron was assured that justice would be meted out. He was able to talk coherently in about fifteen minutes. During that time the gendarme stood with pencil poised ready to take down notes or call for more gendarmes in case the situation grew worse.

Seeing that he had calmed down sufficiently to converse, the head waiter asked, "Your pardon, sir, but were you visited with bodily harm by that atrocious waiter? I assure you that we stand ready to meet any reasonable financial settlement, provided that we can keep it out of the daily journals."

"Name of a cabbage!" the diner answered. "I was not attacked. I can take care of myself. I was a soldier in the Third Empire. What is bodily harm to a man who fought the Prussian Guard in '71?"

With that he became more violent and was led out by a new convoy of gendarmes, who escorted him, with some concerted effort, to a hospital. Going out the door, he shrieked, "He brought the prunes in backward! He brought the prunes in backward!"

Questioning of the frightened waiter seemed to verify this charge. He said everything seemed normal until he served the prunes. The patron looked at them in an amazed manner, clutched at his own throat before making a grasp for the waiter's neck, and screamed, "They're backward! Name of a pig, they are not forward!"

Such was the case. There was no doubt that the prunes had been served the wrong end to. It showed fine discrimination on the part of the patron that he had been possessed of the keen eyesight necessary to detect this colossal blunder. As for myself, since that time I have examined many prunes, both en masse and singly, but I have never been able to tell when one was backward or forward.

I have merely cited this incident to indicate the fine point to which dining in the old country has been drawn. The slightest error is detected by an epicure, and resented.

My time being over, I was then sent to the Café de Marguery to get the hang of the famous sauce. It required two months of close application in the kitchens before I felt qualified to say that I had absorbed the technical details of fillet of sole with sauce Marguery. During those entire sixty days, for fifteen hours a day I experimented with sole and sauce, until I managed at last to produce a combination which was voted perfect by a jury of seven master chefs. It was a dish that even a Brady might sop or a dunker dunk.

Chapter 4

Cooking in a Foreign Language

Rewards followed swiftly. I was loaned by the Café de Marguery to the Palais des Champs-Elysées as a visiting cook, the occasion being a dinner in honor of King Oscar of Sweden. I was there to prepare the sauce Marguery for the King. It was the proudest moment of my life. It seems strange that I could absolutely forget three years of intensive training in a law school, and a good law school, too, and become a heart-and-soul chef. That was what I had finally evolved into. My entire life was bound up and centered in preparing the sauce Marguery for King Oscar. I felt that I was treading on air. The air itself would have been a stable foundation when word was sent back that the King's favorite dish was filet mignon Hederer.

But I knew how to prepare filet mignon Hederer and was permitted to assist another chef in the cooking. Here is the recipe exactly as we wrote it down that day:

> Carefully trim a tenderloin of beef. Cut in small steaks and fry in butter. Lay on each the soft part of stewed oysters. Garnish with blanched marrow. Serve with sauce Bordelaise and cèpes, adding a pinch of finely chopped parsley.

It is a dish worthy of a king. For this I was personally decorated by the French Government with the Cordon Bleu and made an honorary member of the Société des Cuisiniers de Paris. I was the only American to be thus honored at that time, and, for all I know, may still be the only one. This was the fine courtesy extended by a grateful government to a guest chef in Paris in recognition of my efforts to learn the secrets of French cooking. I cabled my good fortune to my father, who answered with congratulations and instructions to proceed with the second stage of my journey.

There may be some people who do not understand the meaning of the word "cèpes" used in the recipes I have given. Cèpes are of the family of mushrooms. They are a delicacy in France and they grow as wild in that country as whiskers do in Russia. They are more easily distinguished from the toadstool than is our own mushroom because they are of a darker color and have a flatter top. They say that the way to tell a mushroom from a toadstool is to eat it. If you live, it's a mushroom. It may surprise folks to know that cèpes grow in the woods. Since earliest boyhood we have been warned that a mushroom found in our woods is a toadstool. A cèpes farmer must depend on his eyesight and luck, as they grow at random in the forests of France and there is no set rule for discovering them.

But a cèpes collector is well off when compared with the truffle agriculturist. For the truffle is the queerest animal in the vegetable kingdom. It is of the genus Tuber. The mushroom belongs to the same family, although the truffle, like a famous American jewelry firm, has absolutely no connection with any other firm of the same name. This subterranean flower is a fleshy, fungous structure and prized as a garniture for highly seasoned dishes. When you chop up the truffle and throw it in goose liver that has been well mashed, and then stir the dish up, you have pâté de foie gras, a name which has probably puzzled many diners.

It was the custom of Rector's to import pâté de foie gras directly from Strasburg, in Alsace-Lorraine. The truffle is found in the southern section of France around Angouleme, not far from Bordeaux. It grows in clayey, sandy soil and gives absolutely no indication of its presence. It has no stem, no buds, no leaves, and no roots. It is just a gob in the ground, a few inches below the surface.

There is no man on earth who can detect the presence of a truffle. Directions for unearthing them are as vague as for discovering gold, which is where you find it. But there is a friend of man who has a keen nose for the elusive truffle, and that friend is the hog. The hog is passionately fond of the truffles and never fails to root them up.

The farmer allows the pig to run at large, and when the pig starts to root he unleashes a trained pack of truffle hounds, who proceed to drive the faithful porker away from the buried treasure. Thereupon a fierce battle follows, with the hog determined to stick to his truffle by premier rights of discovery and conquest. However, the dogs always win, and having no flair of their own for truffles, the queer-looking plant is added to the farmer's crop.

You may think that the expression "truffle hound" is merely a pleasantry, but such animals actually exist in France and are highly prized by the peasants. A truffle about the size of an orange is worth about ten dollars on the hoof. They are prepared for the American market by being packed in brandy, or at least they were formerly prepared this way. As a good sauce is always nine tenths of the dish, you can well imagine that truffle in brandy was not without its steadfast adherents. As I have been retired now for the past eight years, I do not know whether any truffles have been arrested for having brandy in their possession. I never cared much for them myself, as they tasted something like a well-worn rubber heel. Truffles, terrapin, lobster, canvasback, imported fillet of sole, and other fancy dishes gradually got so on the Rectors' nerves that it was nothing unusual for us to sneak out the back way disguised as tourists and plunge into a white-tile restaurant for good old flapjacks and a thousand on a dish.

Jumping on the Grapes

I had learned all that was possible of Parisian cuisine. I now packed my bags and took a train for the southern part of France, my destination being the Bordeaux district, where the finest of vintage grapes are raised. The Bordeaux sector is the vineyard for the world's best wines. I was to spend six months here, studying the making of champagnes and other wines. It was very interesting, as my duties called for tasting practically every famous wine on the list. As I consider this too late a day for anybody to take offence, I can tell you that the Bordeaux grape is not squeezed in a press. The juice is forced out by the bare feet of the French peasants, man, woman, and child, who jump up and down on the grapes. The jumping effect of the grape seems to be transmitted along with the wine itself, because I have often seen men under its influence busily engaged in jumping on one another.

The reason for the pressing by bare feet is that machinery would not only crush the grapes but also crush the seeds, and one seed in a vat of wine would spoil the entire vat. The seed is bitter and a wine buyer could detect the presence of one hundredth of a seed in a hogshead of wine. This is why the peasants jump on the grapes in their bare feet. They work in a big trough and I can still see the juice bubbling up between their toes.

The squeezed juice is drawn off into a lower trough and then pumped up by hand into a tremendous vat. Then all the refuse, the grape skins, leaves, vine, and dregs, are shoveled on top the wine in the vat, where the mass sinks to the bottom. Then through the slow process of fermentation the entire matted bulk is forced to the top of the vat. It forms a crust over the top. This crust becomes as hard and as solid as a parquet floor. I have seen men walking on it.

The wine cools off under its odd lid for a month. Samples are then drawn off and sipped by the wine merchants of Bordeaux and England for appraisal. At one time the wine merchants of America also took part in this ceremony. Bids are offered and refused or granted. The highest bidder often buys in the contents of five or six large vats and barrels it for shipment to Bordeaux. There it is sold again, or bottled, and the output of that season is known by the name of the district and also recognized by the imprint of the year it was made.

The price of the wine also is fixed at the first testing at the vat, although, of course, the price would increase as the wine grew older year by year in the storehouse. I can give you an idea of the size of the vat when I inform you that the contents of four or five might amount to something just below 2,000 barrels.

Chef and Guest of Honor

I bought no wine, as the American trade was monopolized by three or four big interests.

I thought that I had learned all I could about the wine industry and cabled my father for leave to come home. I had been in France so long that I spoke the language perfectly, which accomplishment was to be a big help to me in separating the dollar from its American owner who likes a foreign accent with his food. I was glad to be headed for home again. Lest you think that my six months in the Bordeaux district was an orgy on wine, I will state that though I was cited by the French Government for my cooking in

Paris, I won no medals for my drinking in Bordeaux. Although you might claim that a small boy in an apple tree was not up there to study botany, yet all the wine I tasted was merely for science and research.

I suspect that I sampled many hundreds of vintages in southern France. I was glad that the ordeal was over. I took the boat for America and bade farewell to France, having been the happy recipient of all the honors ever bestowed on an American chef. In order that my dexterity in making sauce Marguery should not languish through lack of practice, I received permission from the boat steward to use his ovens on the trip. The dish was much relished by the passengers, although there was an unusual amount of seasickness for a smooth, pleasant voyage. However, I had ample confidence in my mastery over the sauce and looked forward to new laurels and glory in my native land.

I landed in America in triumph, having gained more honors single-handed than General Pershing did with two million soldiers. I was the sole American carrying the secrets of centuries of European civilization. I was greeted on the wharf by Rector's Russian Orchestra, my father and Diamond Jim Brady, whose first words were, "Have you got the sauce?"

An elaborate dinner was tendered to me that evening by my father. I was the guest of honor and also the cook. First, I prepared the dinner and then sat down with the other guests, who included Sam Shubert, newly arrived from Syracuse, and just starting to show his strength against the famous combine of Klaw & Erlanger. Dan Reed, the tinplate king, Alfred Henry Lewis, of Wolfville fame, Marshall Field, Adolphus Busch, Victor Herbert, John Philip Sousa were present, and, of course, our old friend Jim Brady.

I prepared fillet of sole with sauce Marguery. Diamond Jim dipped a spoon into it, sipped it, smacked his lips and said, "It's so good I could eat it on a Turkish towel."

Here is the recipe for the sauce Marguery—given entirely from memory:

> First, you must use none but imported sole from the English Channel, which must be shipped over alive in tanks. Cut the fillet with a very sharp knife. There are four fillet to a fish. Take the rest of the fish and put them into a big boiler with plenty of leeks, onions, carrots, turnips, lettuce, romaine, parsley, and similar vegetables. The whole mass is reduced by boiling from eight to twelve hours. This leaves a very small quantity of a jellylike substance, which is the essence of the fish. If properly prepared, only a handful of jelly will be obtained from two hundred fish.
>
> In another pan we place the yolks of four dozen eggs. Work a gallon of melted butter into this, stopping every ten minutes to pour in a pint of dry, white wine of good Bordeaux quality. Add from time to time a spoonful of the essence of fish. This is stirred in and cooked in a double boiler in the same way as you would make hollandaise sauce.
>
> Strain the sauce through a very fine sieve. Season with a dash of cayenne and salt. At no time in the preparation of the sauce should it be allowed to come to a boil.
>
> Now we take the fillet, which should be kept on ice to retain their freshness until the sauce is ready. Place them in a pan with just sufficient water to float them a little. About half an inch of water should be sufficient to cover them. After they boil for ten or fifteen minutes, remove and place on a silver platter.

Garnish the dish on one end with small shrimp and on the other end with imported mussels from northern France.

Pour a liberal amount of the sauce over the whole platter. Sprinkle with chopped parsley and place on the grill for the purpose of allowing it to simmer to a golden brown. Then serve.

The Café De Paris Crown Jewel

This completes the famous dish, known throughout the world, which Marguery himself not only created but served to patrons for fifty years. It created a sensation in New York, although I never guaranteed that you could follow Diamond Jim's advice and eat it on a Turkish towel. That's rather a large assignment, and I advise ambitious eaters of table linen and dry goods to start in by first trying to eat the sauce on an ordinary doily. If successful in that they can then try a napkin and work up by easy stages to a Turkish towel.

I followed up the sauce Marguery with crab meat Mornay, which I learned to prepare in the kitchens of the Café de Paris. If Marguery could be digested on a Turkish towel, then Mornay would have been palatable between a sandwich consisting of a doormat and a horse blanket. The recipe is very simple:

> Every housewife knows how to make a rich cream sauce using butter, flour, and cream. After the cream sauce is prepared, place it in the oven and allow it to get so hot that it will brown on the top.
>
> Immediately remove this thin crust from the top with a spoon or ladle. While the sauce is very hot, add small pieces of fresh, sweet

butter, stirring very rapidly. Also add a liberal quantity of grated Swiss cheese. The whole secret of the sauce is constant stirring, the butter and cheese being added alternately.

When the cream sauce, the cheese, and the butter have become well blended, which should take a good fifteen minutes of steady whipping, strain through a fine sieve and season with cayenne and salt.

Pour over large individual flakes of crab meat and allow it to brown under the grill. Serve on a silver platter without garnishing.

All good Americans may go to Paris to die, but not one of them goes there to diet. Crab meat Mornay was the crown jewel of the Café de Paris and no tourist had seen Paris until he had tasted this dish. I have given you recipes for two dishes, which are also recipes for success, because they added over a million dollars to the Rector fortune.

A big wager was laid out in Chicago that a man couldn't eat a quail every day for a month. The betters were James Gore, of Chapin and Gore, and Freddy Stanley, who was Nat Goodwin's closest friend. Chapin and Gore were the big wine merchants of Chicago. Stanley essayed to eat one quail a day for a month and gave up after the twenty-third day. Yet I have seen Charles Frohman and Charles Dillingham eat crab meat Mornay every night for weeks, months, and years.

A Cure for an Epicure

This may have been due to the superiority of the French cuisine and the marvelous ability of the French to disguise dishes with sauces. In fact, they carried out their ingenuity to such an extreme as to befuddle many an epicurean. There is a time in every peak hour in the restaurant business which resembles that minute in a family dinner when unexpected visitors had arrived and the cry, "F.H.B." went up. "F.H.B." was a secret code, which meant that some particular dish was running low and, out of consideration for the visitors' appetites, it could be deciphered to mean "family hold back."

When that moment arrived in some restaurants, and a patron ordered a dish which was on the menu card but not in the kitchen, it was often the proprietor's habit to employ a substitute disguised in sauces. Rector's practiced this deception only once, and then because of a wager. The victim was Dave Montgomery of the famous team of Montgomery and Stone, then playing in their success, *The Red Mill*.

Stone was a very plain eater while Montgomery was an epicurean. Fred grew tired of hearing Dave boast about the many complicated dishes he enjoyed in Rector's on his nightly visits after the show, and especially of his love for the diamond-back terrapin.

He determined to teach the epicurean a lesson. He conferred with me, and, much to Dave's surprise, agreed to accompany him to Rector's to share a dish of terrapin. After the meal, Dave said, "George, this diamond-back terrapin is the finest I have ever tasted."

A roar of laughter from Stone was followed with the explanation that the diamond-back terrapin was nothing but small pieces of stewed rabbit in sauce Maryland. The meat of the rabbit hidden in the sauce is similar to terrapin and the deception is completed by the very small bones which are found both in rabbit and in terrapin. I do not doubt that many a confiding patron has paid for a terrapin which is still swimming in Chesapeake Bay while a mournful rabbit waits in vain for its mate.

Another easy counterfeiting process is substituting milk-fed veal for chicken à la King. The veal is chopped into small chunks and mixed in with an equal quantity of chicken in very much the same way as the famous butcher prepared his half-and-half sausage with half a pig and half a mule.

There are more queer things hidden under sauce than there are under the canvas of a circus.

Another trick employed by unscrupulous restaurateurs is flaking halibut to resemble crab meat. Once again the sauce is the camouflage. I forgot to mention that all these sauces are laced with sherry or Madeira, which completely dominates the diner's palate.

A prime fillet of lamb, marinated in claret, could fool anybody who has the habit of ordering venison stew out of season. And the lamb has the advantage of always being in season. The next time you order venison ask the waiter to bring you the antlers.

Even then, devotees of the canvasback, king of water fowl, think they are certifying their choice when the canvasback is brought in with a real canvasback head on the platter. However, in nine cases out of ten the head is canvasback while the body is mallard. One canvasback head will often act as honorary pall bearer at the gastronomic rites of a hundred mallards. The difference in price in my time was two dollars for the mallard and four dollars for the canvasback, which will not touch fish but lives on wild rice and celery. Once again, a sauce of brandy helped to dull the diner's sense of taste.

Sauce for the Geese

The reputation of Rector's was of such a high standard that we would never dare to attempt a deception. I learned how to make these synthetic dishes while talking with numerous chefs in Paris. They are secrets of the trade. "What is sauce for the goose is sauce for the gander" is an old adage that should never be brought into the kitchen.

In spite of the fact that two sauces made Rector's more than a million dollars, I think that the diner who lets complicated sauces alone and sticks to plain broils and roasts is better off and has fewer liver complaints in the long run. Furthermore, he gets roast beef when he orders it, and not a concoction of cracker-dust gravy and anchovies that might have been prepared on a stove or gathered up in a carpet sweeper.

Chapter 5

Eight Bells on Broadway

There may be some readers of this book who, like a bee on a paper flower, may stop to wonder what it is all about. Why all this fuss and feathers over one extinct restaurant that has evaporated into the limbo of the forgotten, when where were thousands of restaurants and will be thousands more?

We pick out Rector's to speak of for the same reason that Hamlet picked out poor Yorick's skull for a melancholy tête-à-tête. If you remember the play, you will also remember that the Prince of Denmark did not pick up Yorick's entire skeleton to wrestle with. He merely picked up the skull of Yorick, because that was Yorick. And we pick up Rector's restaurant because that was the fountain-head of New York life of the period. The rest didn't matter.

There may be some adherents of Sherry's and Delmonico's who will protest against my claim to gastronomic supremacy of the past. Should they care to throw down the gauntlet of memory, I shall be glad to break a toothpick with them in knightly joust. Rector's did a bigger business than either one of these two famous establishments. But I must admit that Sherry's and Delmonico's occupied unique niches in the Hall of Food. Both these restaurants drew upon the same clientele, the Four Hundred. Rector's not only attracted the Four Hundred but also most of O. Henry's beloved Four Million. It was the spot where Broadway and Fifth Avenue met.

Incidentally, I was instrumental in helping O. Henry to write a story which he never wrote. At least, I have read every one of his stories many times and have never been able to discover the one to which I refer. He was an infrequent visitor to our place, as he preferred to dine in quiet, odd places. Our place was odd, but not quiet. When he came in, he always picked out a table in the corner and made himself as inconspicuous as possible. I knew of him, but had never spoken to him, because I always respected a patron's desires, either communicated by words or telegraphed by actions.

There is much psychology connected with the running of successful restaurants, especially one catering to a class consisting of brokers, bankers, merchants, turfmen, actors, and opera singers. We studied the faces of our patrons at the door, and a glance told us whether they were in good, bad, or indifferent humor. A good customer in a bad humor was handled extremely carefully. A man might come into our place with a grouch and imagine that he got it there. The head waiter himself would personally take charge of the disgruntled one and see that he had specially prepared dishes and express service. And I will say that it required an extra-fine dish to make a man forget that he had just finished a disastrous day in Wall Street or a singer that she was an octave below Metropolitan Opera caliber.

The evening I spoke to O. Henry was the one on which he spoke to me first. He sent the waiter to me with a request that I come over to his table. I was delighted, because the man's fame had already taken hold of the nation and his genius was recognized even by those writers who thought they were his rivals. He had no rivals. He introduced himself, which I assured him was unnecessary.

He asked rather abruptly, "Have you a marine clock on your yacht?" I assured him that we had, and he then inquired, "Can you explain to me the striking of the bells?"

I told him that the even bells were on the hour and the odd on the half hour. In other words, two bells meant one o'clock, while three bells were 1:30. He didn't quite grasp this, or he must have had his mind made up to something definite, because he said, "Are eight bells eight o'clock?"

I told him yes, but that eight bells were not only eight but also four and twelve. He said, "That's what I wanted to know. Thank you."

He then inquired whether ship's time ran from one o'clock to twenty-four around the clock or from one to twelve. I told him that marine time was from one to twelve. He then asked, "Would a man in a dark room, hearing a marine clock chime eight bells, know whether it was morning, noon, or night?"

I did not grasp the idea of his questioning, but was delighted to assist him in any manner. I informed him that a man in a dark room who heard a ship's clock strike eight bells would not know whether it was night or day by the sound of the bells alone. He said, "Here is the idea. . . . Sit down."

I had been standing up until that time, as it was not the policy of Rector's to sit with patrons. Sometimes I did so upon request, but very rarely. It was the training of restaurants of our type to feel that you were a public servant and to act the role throughout. Not one of our patrons ever had to remind one of our waiters that he was a waiter or myself that I was there to look after his comfort.

The Story O. Henry Never Wrote

But this was an extraordinary occasion and I drew up a chair gladly, even proudly. O. Henry continued: "I require some technical information. A man is found murdered in a cheap tenement house far in the heart of New York. No one in the house knows anything about him except the landlady, who remembers one solitary visitor of a Latin-American type who came around about two or three times a year. Each visit was the signal for violent quarrelling, and the slamming of a door when the South American departed. After one of these visits and an unusually violent argument, the man is found dead in his room the next morning. The visitor is picked up on the landlady's testimony to the police that she heard the sounds of a blow, the falling of a body, and the slamming of a door just as the clock struck eight.

"The South American claims that at eight o'clock he was in a barroom on the water front and brings witnesses to prove it. Of course, you understand that I am jumping rapidly and we are now at the trial of the accused man. He is about to be convicted on the landlady's testimony, when his lawyer—he has a lawyer, of course, because it develops that he is the agent for a rich banana republic on the Isthmus—his lawyer brings in last-minute evidence that the landlady's testimony is worthless because the striking of the clock meant nothing! It struck eight all right, but the striking was eight bells, which not only could have been eight p.m. but also eight a.m. And in addition it could have meant four in the morning, four in the afternoon, or noon or midnight. It was a ship's clock."

O. Henry scratched his head a trifle, and then said: "There's one thing I forgot. Even with the striking of eight bells the landlady would have been able to tell whether it was day or night, because, though the windows in tenements are dirty, they are never that dirty. I will have to make the landlady blind, and I hate to do that, because landladies are my best friends—when I have the rent. . . . Thank you very much, Mr. Rector."

When Ignorance is Golden

I assured him that it was a pleasure to have been of any service, and arose. As I said before, I have never run across that story in the collected works of O. Henry. If any of my readers know about it, I would be glad to hear from them. I do not think that he ever wrote it. He may have discarded the idea as being too involved or because he was too soft-hearted to deprive even an imaginary landlady of her sight. He may have started the tale and never finished it.

Like all brilliant minds, he worked on impulse as spasmodic as the last kick of a dying frog. The magazines which bought his work were compelled to keep after him continually to obtain the fruit of their advance payments. He was a dreamer and not one-hundredth part of his stories were ever placed on paper. This seems to have been one of them. It is to my sorrow that I must say I was never his intimate except on this occasion, which was undoubtedly due to the fact that O. Henry had either heard or read about my father's yacht, the *Atlantic,* which we had purchased from Wilson Marshall, who afterward built the three-masted schooner yacht of the same name and won the transatlantic race for the Kaiser's Cup. It was a magnificent gold emblem of the jeweler's craft.

Mr. Marshall was a member of the New York Yacht Club and no trophy was ever treasured as this one. It sparkled and glistened in the sunlight like a tarpon breaking water under the aurora borealis. It was the most magnificent cup I have ever seen, and the presentation of such a solid-gold gift must have eaten heavily into the imperial strong box. However, all patriotic Americans will remember the glorious day when this cup was considered contraband of red-white-and-blue emotions and was condemned by its owner to ignoble auction. A test was made to determine its ultimate sales price and it was found to be the cheapest of pewter!

The gold, like all other beauty, was but skin deep. All the rest was junk. There is no doubt that if the New York Yacht Club had discovered this ten years sooner, the World War would have occurred ten years earlier in history. The *Atlantic* footed it so fast in the race that won the Kaiser's Cup that rival foreign yachtsmen suspected her of using her engine room. She was an auxiliary schooner; but before the race her engine room was sealed and her propeller unshipped. She had coal bunkers, but no coal, and the cup she won would have made a fine auxiliary coal scuttle.

One of Mr. Marshall's closest friends was Augustus W. Mott, of the Mott Iron Works, a millionaire many times over, though he never owned a yacht. He died one of the richest bachelors in the United States, thus attaining two remarkable records of that period. One was to die rich, the other was to die a bachelor. He often sailed with Mr. Marshall on the first *Atlantic* before my father bought it. It was not equipped with an auxiliary engine, and once, when becalmed among the lobster pots off Rhode Island, Mr. Mott suggested that he be allowed the loan of a rowboat and a couple of sailors.

Not knowing just what his guest had in mind, Mr. Marshall humored his request and was astonished to see the newly created admiral of a rowboat direct his four-oared armada up to a lobster pot buoy and then start to pull up the pot. His crew endeavored to dissuade him, as trifling with a lobster trap off the waters of Rhode Island is equivalent to suggesting to a movie fan that the famous dog Rin-Tin-Tin would make good frankfurters. It is lese majesty of the finest kind and punishable by a preparatory course in jail and a fat penalty in dollars.

Nevertheless, Mr. Mott pulled up the pot, picked a half-dozen buds from the beautiful bouquet of clawing green and deposited them in the rowboat. Then he placed twenty dollars, a good cigar, and his calling card in the lobster pot, lowered the pot, and was rowed in triumph back to the Atlantic. After the finish of the cruise, Mr. Mott returned to his beautiful home on Fifth Avenue, refreshed in mind and body. There was a letter awaiting him, post-marked Rhode Island. It was from the bereaved owner of the six lobsters and read:

Dear Mr. Mott: Thanks. Call again.

The twenty dollars probably consoled the fisherman for the absence of the lobsters and the presence of the cigar. Mr. Marshall raced his boats all over the world, but never had the good fortune to compete with Sir Thomas Lipton. But they were very good friends, either ashore or afloat. Sir Thomas visited Rector's very often and was fond of Virginia ham, a delicacy not obtainable on the other side. We cooked it for him in champagne sauce. He celebrated all his international victories at Rector's and he did not drink tea. I might add that he had good judgment enough to celebrate all his victories in advance.

Where Good Yachtsmen Got Together

He was usually accompanied by Sir John Dewar, who always made the speeches for the taciturn Lipton. Sir Thomas was rather bashful about after-dinner speeches, while Sir John loved them. He was a good talker, too, and very humorous. I remember one of his lines which has been appropriated by many of our own speakers. In finishing a talk, he said: "And now, like Lady Godiva, after a short but interesting journey, I approach my close." The play on the word "clothes" was, of course, the key to the joke. Sir John didn't drink tea, either.

There was a yachting table in our place where famous and luxurious navigators used to gather. Among these men were Howard Gould, owner of the famous *Niagara;*

Commodore Cornelius Vanderbilt, Col. James Elverson, Lloyd Phoenix, Harry Harkness, Commodore Mills, and many others who might saunter casually out of Rector's and make a trip around the world before sauntering just as casually in again.

There was another class of yachtsmen who frequented Rector's but who never sat down at the yachting table. These globe-trotters were known as deep-sea promoters. They were suave, well-groomed gentlemen who spoke three or four languages perfectly. In fact, their lingual accomplishments were far superior to those of our good old friend Sam Bernard, who, when asked during the World War if he spoke German, said, "Fluently, but not lately."

These ocean salesmen were famous workers in their line. Like the man who, in organizing a transatlantic passenger line, promised to supply the ocean, provided that his proposed partner furnished the boats, they had little stock in trade. In fact, they had even less than this shoe-string promoter, because the ships were there, Nature supplied the water, and all they gave was their illustrious presence. They were tub workers.

In this case, "tub worker" did not mean bending over the week's wash in the back of a Chinese laundry. This group of tourists worked the tubs. The tubs were ocean liners. Their polish was as false as the sheen on an oiled apple. It could be dropped readily, and in passing their tables I often overheard such sinister words as "the mouthpiece," "the big store," "the mob," "the iron theatre," and "the rap."

This may mean nothing to you unless I explain that the mouthpiece was a lawyer, the big store was the district attorney's office, the mob was a gang of crooks, the iron theatre was a jail, and the rap was either an accusation or a term in jail. They were not nice lads, but there was no way of excluding them provided they behaved themselves.

And they always acted very well in Rector's. They were good company outside of office hours. They never tried any tricks in New York, as they were exporters, not importers. I knew them all, having met them in Paris while I was working as a cook in the kitchens of the Café de Paris.

When I finished with my work in the evening, I would discard my apron, coat, and white chefs cap and put on my dinner suit. Quite a transformation for a slinger of hash. Then I would stroll over to the Café Tourtelle, which was directly opposite the Grand Café on the Boulevard des Italiens. The Café Tourtelle was the rendezvous for American confidence men in Paris. They would meet there between sailings of the boats and, if they had had a successful trip over, they would continue on to Monte Carlo to drop their hardly earned money. Not hard earned, but hardly.

It is an odd thing to know that the shearers of sheep on the high seas were contributors of fleece to the Prince of Monaco. They all came away from the spinning tables well shorn. If they picked up any money on the return trip to America, there wasn't a doubt that they would lose their illicit gainings at roulette tables in New York or Saratoga.

Among these men were such notorious characters as Shang Draper, Bud Hauser, Doc Waterbury, and Doc Owens. They were the most prominent of the capable gypsies, who could not only tell fortunes by cards but reduce those fortunes in the telling. They are all dead now. One of them was buried at sea, which meant that the nimble fingers had hesitated for just the fatal instant that was enough to enlighten the prospective victim and convert him into an enraged destroyer with a ready gun. There may have been an investigation of Bud Hauser's death, but it never reached shore. Neither did Bud Hauser. He could well have been added to the song of the Lord High Executioner of the Mikado as a person who would never be missed.

These gentlemen worked in unison, a mob generally consisting of three or four men and, in many cases, a beautiful woman. When booking passage overseas, they always travelled separately and rarely spoke to one another until the second or third day at sea, a time when speaking to a fellow passenger was as natural as conversing with a relative. Their line of procedure in netting a victim was well routined. It was divided into a campaign of three distinct tableaux. The first was known as the approach. In the approach, one of the gang scraped a chatting acquaintance with the victim on the second or third day out. After a pleasant conversation and an agreement to meet at dinner, the shark would go to his cabin and keep out of sight for a day. In the meantime, a second member of the manipulating clique would approach the same victim and also become very friendly. The result was that the victim would find himself with two good friends.

While talking to one of these gentlemen on the fourth day, the other would stroll up and the victim would introduce them to each other. This is one of the best approaches, as the victim imagined he was introducing two perfect strangers. They may have been strangers, but they were not perfect. There are many approaches, but this one will be a clew to the others. The others of the gang would be introduced to one another, and in every case the victim would be the man who did the introducing.

The Partridgers' Famous Party

Pleasant hours of intelligent and amusing conversation would follow, which would gradually lead into the build-up. The build-up was just what its name implies, a building up of the victim into a proper frame of mind for cards or dice. Either way, he had about as much chance as a steer in a cattle car. The gang had his history, knew that he would gamble and was not above being willing to accept a slight edge on the other fellow.

The rich victim was generally taken in as a partner of the gang, who assured him that another member of the card party was a wealthy fish who could afford to lose a hundred thousand and enjoy it. The game would start small and gradually grow as the end of the voyage approached. Or it might start in casino, bridge, or pinochle and suddenly switch to that noblest of all American substitutes for insomnia—stud poker.

The victim always won until the time came for the hoorah. The hoorah should be flanked by an escort of honor consisting of many exclamation points. It was very sudden and never occurred until the last night out. The heir to the hoorah was the victim. He could inherit the hoorah in many ways, as there were numerous tricks in the bag known as the late hour.

I will explain this by saying that the late hour meant that nothing crooked was attempted until a late hour, when the quarry was befuddled by too much smoking, possibly too much drinking and too continuous a strain on his physical stamina. His eye would be dulled and his mind numbed and he would be in no condition to combat the wiles of the gang. In fact, he wouldn't be looking for anything wrong from such good friends. By the time he woke up the next morning they would be off the boat. The realization that they had let him in on a scheme to fleece another man would usually compel him to keep his mouth closed.

It's a wise man who never gambles with strangers. It's a wiser man who never gambles with his friends. All other vices are virtues compared with the vice of gambling. It will put a man in the gutter faster than anything else and take his wife and children with him. Once acquired, it is never broken, and there is an old saying in New York that the doctors support Wall Street and the actors support the race track. Although I never gambled, I was often host to many gambling soirées. We made a practice of renting our private dining rooms to private parties consisting of four people or more. The card games in Rector's private rooms were started by society folks who preferred our place to their homes because of the excellent food and service.

If there are any of my readers who have ever helped to feed a three-dollar kitty for sandwiches and light in a friend's home, they will be staggered to learn that the kitty in Rector's often reached $1,100 or $1,200. More of a roaring tiger than a kitty. Gambling would not be allowed in private dining rooms in any restaurant in America to-day.

The Partridge Club also met every Friday night for years in the seclusion of one of our private rooms. This club was named after its own famous partridge dinners. It was one of the most exclusive poker clubs in New York City. They played a straight twenty-dollar limit. After the poker game they would sit in for table-stakes stud. Pots of $20,000 and $30,000 were nothing unusual. The members of the Partridge Club were not professional gamblers. They were wealthy business men, many of whom are still alive. Tiring of stud poker they might turn to bridge for fifty cents and a dollar a point.

I have attended, catered to, and heard of many dinners, but the one that burns brightest in memory was one given by the Partridgers. It was a dinner of boneless shad! Thousands of indignant housewives may rise up and protest that there is no such animal on land or sea. Millions of diners, who had eaten countless numbers of bread crusts in painful efforts to accelerate the passage of a shad bone through the throat, may accuse me of deliberate falsehood. But Rector's served the Partridge Club boneless shad. The only recipe necessary was a shad, a magnifying glass, and the genius that is a capacity for infinite pains. We served six shad at that dinner and it took eight cooks all day to pick the bones out of the fish. From that day to this, I have been a great admirer of jellyfish, sponges, watermelons, and other food without backbones, ribs, or bones. That night the kitty was a leopard.

Chapter 6

The Contract with a Washout

Rector's was in no way associated with gambling. Although Dick Canfield often ate there, he never touched a card. He ran the famous Canfield's next door to Delmonico's, where one New York society man dropped $200,000 in a night. I knew Canfield a year before I knew he was the professional gambler. The same for Davy Johnson, who thought nothing of betting $250,000 on an election. They were nothing like the popular conception of gamblers. No one ever went from our main dining room into a private room to gamble. All parties were selected by the host and included his personal friends only. But at the same time that this occurred in Rector's, the police were raiding corner saloons and arresting sailors for shaking dice for five-cent beers.

However, there was gambling in the main dining room. But it was the kind of hazard that is recognized as legitimate. It was the rise and fall of the tides of Wall Street. Brokers and traders would give commissions over their midnight coffee for thousands of shares. We were once compelled to keep a linen napkin in our office safe overnight because of a memorandum written on it in lead pencil. It was a contract calling for the transfer of 5,000 shares of a certain railroad stock, then selling at $80 a share. When we sent that napkin to the laundry, we sent one of the signers with it, for he was cleaned, too. He guaranteed to deliver at 75 and the stock opened the next morning at 82 and rose six points more, closing at 88.

The stock plunger whom I remember best of all was the one and only Brandt Walker. He was a heavy trader in stocks and also a better in the same flimsy material. His favorite bet was the "Up-five-before-down-five." This bet was made after the market closed in the afternoon. We will say that the stock in question is steel, selling at $90 a share at the closing of the daily market. Brandt Walker was always bearish and I have seen him bet $20,000 that this stock would reach 85 the next day before it reached 95. This was what gave it the title of "Up-five-before-down-five." In Walker's case it should have been reversed, for he always bet down.

He came on from Chicago practically broke. He made his money in the panic of 1907 by selling short of the market. He was down at Lakewood, New Jersey, for a short vacation and directed his selling from a broker's office in a hotel at that resort. He cleaned up $3,000,000. His father caught the next train from Chicago, took away $1,000,000 from his boy and purchased him an annuity. The older Walker was a prominent corporation lawyer of Chicago. The sageness of parental counsel was validated when Brandt was cleaned out a short time later. The remaining $2,000,000 was speedily lost and there were markers against Brandt for many thousands of dollars. However, neither his creditors nor himself could touch the principal of the annuity, because an annuity is non-attachable. And only Brandt could collect the annuity. Twice a year there was paid into his hand $25,000 in gold. He lived long enough to collect his annuity for almost twenty years, and probably died thinking that he was smarter than his father.

Fortunes were made and lost over the tablecloths in Rector's in legitimate business deals. It was during these times that a day-and-night bank was first established so that a railroad could be bought outside of Wall Street and banking hours! It was a long time before the ticker stopped sobbing over that coup.

Before the Boom

At this period real estate in Times Square was still an unknown quantity. When Rector's started at Forty-fourth and Broadway, there were no subway kiosks. Pedestrians did not pop in and out of the ground like gophers in the Dakotas. We were in the middle of Long Acre Square. Where the Knickerbocker Hotel now stands was the old St. Cloud Hotel. Incidentally, the Knickerbocker is now an office building. Every time I look at it I think of Armistice Day, when the shouting and tumult died away as Caruso appeared on the balcony of his top-floor apartment and sang the national anthems of America, France, and Italy.

Across from the St. Cloud, on Broadway, was the famous Metropole Hotel, which, losing its lease, moved to Forty-third Street, just east of Broadway, and was the scene of the shooting of Rosenthal, for which a police lieutenant and four gunmen went to the chair. There were two large rooming houses where the Hotel Astor now stands. Hammerstein's Olympia was to the north of us on the east side of Broadway. It is now known as the New York Theatre. On the northern end of Long Acre Square was the Brewster carriage factory, occupying the site of the present Strand Theatre. Diagonally opposite the square, on Forty-eighth Street, was the Studebaker factory, whose mission in life was the building of bigger and better wagons and buggies. The trend of the traffic was northward, although there were very few theatres in this section.

It remained for a young Philadelphian to come over and realize the hypothetical values in this district. His name was Felix Isman and he rapidly became a power in

Manhattan Island realty. He also became a prominent figure in theatricals and theatrical real estate. One of his biggest deals was put over right in Rector's.

At this period vaudeville was divided east and west. The Keith interests controlled the field as far west as Chicago. All west of Chicago, including Chicago and Cincinnati, was under the banner of Martin Beck and the Orpheum Circuit. The two powerful interests had tacit agreements that neither should invade the other's territory.

One evening Felix was dining in Rector's when Martin Beck walked in, having just dropped off a Chicago train. Beck made some remark about the weather, which was one thing that Felix never argued about. He knew that Beck hadn't travelled the thousand miles from Chicago to become an expert on Eastern weather. He finished his coffee, paid his check, and taking Beck by the arm walked him to the site where the Palace Theatre now stands at Forty-seventh and Broadway.

An Age of Sandwich Snatchers

Pointing to the plot, Felix said, "That's the place for your theatre."

Isman knew that the Orpheum had declared war the minute he saw Beck standing in front of his table in Rector's. Speech is made to conceal thoughts and a remark about the weather may hide much cogitation about real estate. Isman brought his man back to Rector's and sold him the ground. Beck built the Palace Theatre and was bought out later by Mr. Keith. The little deal netted Isman around $800,000 before his yearly bonuses ceased. No gold bonanza ever discovered equaled the surface-gold mining in Times and Long Acre squares.

The Rector plot was 75 feet front on Broadway, with a depth of about 100 feet. There were also two houses on

Forty-fourth Street purchased by my father from Charles T. Barney, the whole forming an ell. The purchase price was $750,000. On the corner of Forty-fourth Street and Broadway stood a building which occupied a plot of twenty-five feet on Broadway, with a depth of only sixty feet. This property we acquired on a sixty-year lease for a rental of $20,000 a year. Just to give you an idea of how values jumped overnight, we immediately placed a mortgage of $1,650,000 on the ground of the proposed Rector Hotel. The property to-day is worth in the neighborhood of $4,000,000.

An idea of rentals in the district can be gleaned from the fact that the entire Rector restaurant paid a rent of only $10,000 a year. On the same spot to-day is a twelve-by-six orange-drink stand paying a reputed rental of $25,000 a year. That orange-drink stand may not seem significant of anything in particular, but it is the real reason why the corner saloon can never come back in America. The soft-drink stand, the cigar store, and the drug store have gobbled up the spots vacated by the barroom and are paying three to five times the rent formerly paid by the saloon keeper. That is one reason why the saloon will never return. There is no place for it. Quite a change from the times spoken of by a friend of mine when he said, "In those old days there was a saloon on every corner. I was born at a place called Five Corners."

The customer in a cigar store does not linger more than fifteen or twenty seconds. He is in and out again. Therefore the cigar store has fifty patrons to the saloon's one. That's one reason why the disappearance of the corner saloon has not left any scar or unhealed wound in the long vista of business properties in your city. When the saloon was jerked out, a newer and better tooth grew in its place. In fact, the saloon's former location on our maps would be as difficult to locate as a pinhole in rubber. Furthermore, business is now all business and no sentiment. We have yet to hear of any customer staggering out of a candy store after having insisted on kissing the soda-water clerk good-night.

If I could open up the Rector restaurant to-day, under no circumstances would I serve liquor. Instead of having one drinking party occupying a table for five hours I would be able to serve ten parties at the same table in the same time. In fact, this generation of ours is not a generation of diners at all. It is a tribe of sandwich grabbers. The cafeterias, the Purple Kitchens, the Busy Bees, and the soda-water fountains supply the business men with their luncheon.

It was only last winter that a certain big hotel rented its ground-floor corner to a drug store. A few months later the same hotel petitioned the courts to restrain the druggist from selling soups, sandwiches, milk, and cake on the premises, claiming that the drug store's fast and furious bargains in light luncheon had irreparably damaged the business of the hotel's dining rooms. The learned judge ruled that it was within the province of the druggist to include ham, cheese, and olives in his staple line of chemicals and nostrums.

But the hotel gained a point when His Honor restrained the druggist from serving hot soups and meals, as the presence of a stove behind the soda-water counter violated the fire laws of the city.

Trained-Seal Etiquette

The best description of modern eating is furnished by the spangled performers of the big tents. In the parlance of the circus lot, dining is known as throwing in. And the business man of to-day literally throws in. Lunch-counter manners are a sort of trained-seal etiquette. The morsel is swished from the plate to the mouth with a sudden parabola of the spoon or fork. Pop! and it's gone. Gulp! and another swift arc of the spoon.

Sometimes I expect the diner to complete the sealish impersonation by balancing an extra fine chunk of meat on his nose, tossing it into the air with a flip of his neck and then catching it in his capable mouth on its downward journey.

The dining of to-day must break the heart of Berry Wall. And I know that it would have driven Ward McAllister insane. Ward was the man who is responsible for the term "Four Hundred," meaning the number of people composing the cream of American society. That small number would be but condensed cream to-day.

Berry Wall was very exacting and fastidious in his dining. When he ordered early June peas he wanted them as carefully matched as Oriental pearls. I have no doubt that Mr. Wall could easily have detected a late May arrival in his group of early June peas. The aroma of food was as important to him as the taste. He also feasted with his eyes, and in ordering his food would describe his dinner to the waiter with sweeping gestures. When he ordered oysters on the half shell he went through a pantomime with his hands indicating the opening of the oysters, their appearance on the shell, arrival at the table, and his disposal of them.

I still remember seeing him order an entire dinner by the wigwag system. He started with the silent drama of the oysters. The waiter observed, but said nothing. Then Berry ordered soufflé of potatoes with cold flakes of crab meat. He indicated the size of the individual flake of crab meat by extending his hand and pressing the nail of his forefinger into the ball of his thumb. The waiter still stood silent but watchful.

Then followed the description of the soufflé in the sign language. He indicated the puffiness by extending the fingers of both hands in much the same manner that a woman tries to catch a baseball. Then he drew both hands together and spread them apart again rapidly, exactly like a musician playing an imaginary accordion. Filling his cheeks, he blew his breath rapidly through his lips to illustrate the desired lightness and puffiness of the soufflé.

He usually stopped to twirl his moustache, brush a crumb off the table linen, roll his lapels and polish his watch with his thumb and forefinger of the right hand. He never actually looked at the watch, but would pull it out of his vest pocket fifteen or twenty times. By this time he would be ready for the supreme effort—the ordering of the *poussang,* or squab chicken. He would run his fingers lightly over the tablecloth, as if he were a famous pianist strumming the keyboard. Then he would reach for his *apéritif,* sip it lightly, place it on the table and inhale deeply. He explained the tenderness of the squab by waving a cigar in his hand like a leader directing an orchestra playing the love motif of Aida. His method of illustrating the plumpness of the squab was to throw out his chest and hold his breath until we thought he would strangle.

He never allowed a waiter to bring a completed salad to the table. He ordered his endives and heart of palm separately. The olive oil was another individual item. So was the vinegar, and also the pepper mill. He kept his own bottle of vinegar in our kitchens just as an old-time member of the Odd Fellows had his private lather mug in the barber shop. This bottle of vinegar was red wine that had turned sour and contained a dozen buttons of garlic. An open bowl of ice was brought in. Inside that bowl was a smaller china bowl, empty, but placed in the larger bowl to attain the proper degree of frostiness.

When the small bowl was thoroughly chilled, he would sprinkle a liberal pinch of paprika over it, then a quarter of a spoonful of mustard and the same quantity of salt. Then he would hold the pepper mill over the dish and turn out ten grinds of pepper. The true epicurean always insisted on grinding his own pepper from the whole pepper berry. If you imagine that Wall was performing the secret rites and incantations of a witch doctor seeking to bring rain to a parched nation, you are wrong. He was simply in the act of mixing his own salad dressing. Then he put in two heaping tablespoonfuls of olive oil, taking extreme care not to allow it to splash. The oil was poured out over the rim of the spoon like a small but important Niagara. Now came his treasured bottle of vinegar. This was allowed to drip in by tilting the bottle in the left hand, meanwhile stirring with the right.

The idea of this formula was to allow the oil to jell when it struck the cold surface of the bowl. By pouring the oil in first, Berry made it smooth and thick and it blended perfectly with the vinegar. He took as much pride in this discovery as a scientist would in the completion of a revolutionizing theory of extracting acid from moonbeams. I can imagine Wall rising to his feet in the midst of the peace negotiations at Versailles, pointing his finger at Lloyd George, Clemenceau, Poincaré and earnestly protesting, "Don't pour the vinegar in first."

Then he would put in the heart of palm and the endives at the same time. With the spoon in the right hand and the fork in the left, he would stir them and scoop them up so that they would absorb the precious dressing. After a few minutes of mixing, he would serve it to himself on his salad dish, which also was chilled. He would eat his salad with some dandy Camembert cheese, running south. By "running south" we meant the cheese was so soft that it had to be eaten with a spoon instead of a knife.

Whenever I met cheese heading in that direction I usually started north.

This is the manner in which a real epicurean dined. Compare this with a frantic patron at a sandwich counter, wolfing his food like the famous Sam White of Princeton spearing a fumbled football on the dead run. Truly, the Earl of Sandwich little dreams of what he started when he invented that cold slice of meat between two blankets of bread.

I forgot to state that after Mr. Berry Wall had spent thirty minutes in gesturing and pantomiming his idea of a dinner to the silent but eagle-eyed waiter, the garçon also qualified for the French school of emotional acting by clapping both hands together twice and jerking the thumb of his right hand back over his shoulder, indicating that the kitchen had been closed for ten minutes before Mr. Wall had started giving his order.

Chapter 7

On Tipping

When launching a French restaurant in New York we tried to reverse that old adage: "The imitator of a man gets all his vices and none of his virtues." What is true of an individual is true also of an institution. There was one vice we sought to circumvent, and that bad habit was the tipping evil.

A man dining in a Paris Café must donate honorariums to at least five or six servants connected with the establishment. The usual fee for the maître d'hôtel was 100 francs in the days when a franc was a franc. In return for this monstrous emolument of office, this individual would assure you that you were looking splendid, that the lady was getting thinner, and it was a fine day. I have bought my weather reports much cheaper in America.

The next solicitor in the Royal Franch Academy of Itching Palms would be the capitaine. A capitaine is a man who is not quite a maître d'hôtel, but is too proud to be a waiter. His fee would be twenty francs and his duties were to lead you to a wabbly table in a desirable spot. He would also take your order and assure you that you were never looking better in your life, even though he had never seen you before.

When the capitaine had taken your order he would then go into executive session with your garçon, whose share of the plunder was at least 10 per cent. of your check. The omnibus, a frail juvenile who carried dishes which were too heavy for the big strong waiters, received his bit of the spoils from the waiter's end of the swag. On your way out you were forced to run the gauntlet of the *vestiaire* and the *chasseur,* known in a less expensive language as the checkroom boy and the starter. All these uniformed mendicants would assure you that you never looked better in your career. I have no doubt that an extra franc would make them reveal the past and foretell the future.

However, our efforts to modulate the tipping epidemic were without avail. It grew and grew until it was out of proportion to the services rendered. I think that Americans like to tip and would regard the abolition of this peculiar form of tribute as a violation of their constitutional rights. Men like Stanford White, Sidney Love, Charles Thorley, Harry Content, Larry Waterbury, Harry Lehr, Morton Plant, and Harry Thaw were liberal tippers.

The prize tipper was the famous Scotty from Death Valley. Scotty came to New York with a bagful of twenty-dollar gold pieces supposed to have been mined in his private El Dorado in Death Valley. When first seated at his table, Scotty would tear a fifty-dollar bill in half. He would then give the waiter the western half of the bill and retain the eastern half, saying, "Now if the service is all right, I will give you the other half." Needless to state, the service was always neat if not gaudy. I have seen Scotty line up the waiters and chefs in Rector's in an *ensemble* resembling a minstrel show. He would then give each one a twenty-dollar gold piece, a total of around $800 or $900.

Frank Gould came in one night between acts of *Zaza,* then being played by Mrs. Leslie Carter at the Criterion. Although not a dramatic critic, Frank had accumulated a headache and asked our head waiter, Paul Perret, for a remedy. Paul suggested a cure known in his native land as kirschwasser, a Swiss cordial. Gould felt better in a few seconds and, before rushing back to the Criterion, he pressed a bill in Paul's hands. It was a $100 tip—about ninety-eight dollars more than Gould would have had to pay a doctor.

Of course, the big take was around the holidays, when the rich patrons of Rector's remembered their favorite waiters with substantial checks. The biggest recipient of Yuletide spirit was the head waiter, who often took down $15,000 or $20,000 in checks. The largest single tip I recall was the one given by Dan Reid, the tin-plate king, to the same Paul Perret. It was not in the form of money, but was a tip to buy Rock Island and hold for a rise. When Perret sold his stock, his profits were $14,000. I consider that the papa of all tips.

Although we thought that a patron of Rector's should enjoy the privilege of checking his hat and coat free, we soon found this was impossible. The first check-room boy was Jerry Pelton, who started working for us at a salary of fifteen dollars a week. Jerry was a very polite and efficient checker of hats and umbrellas, and soon startled us by offering to buy the check-room privileges for $100 a month. We couldn't understand the reason for this and suspected that he might be helping himself to the contents of pockets and high-grading in gold-headed canes. However, when Jerry explained that he wanted to be his own boss, and was in love with the charming little telephone girl, Anna, we sold him the coat-room rights for a year at his own price.

Patrons of Rector's will recall this romance. At the end of the year Jerry had a gold-headed cane and a fur coat of his own to check. By then we began to have some suspicion of the richness of the checking privilege, especially when another youngster offered us $300 a month. Rumors circulated that the check room at Rector's was a bonanza and Jerry was forced to bid $5,000 a year. It grew each season until Jerry was contributing $10,000 a year to Rector's.

The Susskind brothers decided that a hat-and-coat business must be profitable, especially when your customers furnished the hats and coats. So they entered the field and cleaned up $500,000, often paying as much as $15,000 yearly for the coat room in a popular hotel or cabaret. The king of the check rooms to-day is Leon Mollet, who pays fabulous sums for concessions and has grown enormously rich.

Hot Dogs

The concessionaire is a very important man in modern life. He is a sort of fungus growth on the ship of commerce. And, like fungus, he must wait until something is started to which he can cling. He becomes wealthy peddling peanuts at another man's circus, will pay you $500 a month if you can guarantee him exclusive taxicab rights at the front door of your big hotel or restaurant, and would like nothing better than to be the owner of the only hose in a city ablaze. Before he would soak your property, he would soak your pocketbook plenty.

We soon discovered that we must reckon with the concessionaire. Before the new century dawned, we had leased the candy, florist, and souvenir concessions in Rector's; and we also got a substantial sum from a ticket agency for some of our floor space.

The now famous Democratic Convention in Madison Square Garden was a choice bit for the frankfurter concessionaires, who ran the bid up to $10,000. They must have had a good idea of what the delegates liked to eat. Each extra day of the historic deadlock meant the destroying of thousands of frankfurters. When the Garden was torn down last year, there was a report that workmen, excavating in the basement, discovered a secret dungeon in which two loyal delegates sat, chewing hot dogs and shouting "Twenty-four votes for Oscar Underwood!"

Although the job of waiting on tables became a concession in some restaurants, we never allowed this at Rector's, even though this custom existed in some very prominent places, both in France and America. We paid our waiters twenty-five dollars a month. They averaged from $600 to $900 a month in tips. This was rich pickings. Soon we had applicants for waiting jobs who offered to work for nothing. There were some waiters who tried to pay us for the privilege of working in our place. We never hired men like these. We wanted all our men on our payroll; and though we knew our men expected tips, we didn't want to turn timber wolves loose among a pack of polite foxes.

A waiter at Rector's was a salesman, was regarded as such, talked to as such, and never tried to get away from the idea of being merely a waiter. Patrons would come in and look for their same waiter night after night. All our waiters were educated in their profession on the other side and spoke six and seven languages. They had worked in the capitals of the world and on all the big ocean steamers. We found that the best servants were boys who had attended the College of Waiters in Geneva, Switzerland. Never have I seen such waiters in my life. They were polished, subservient, and of handsome appearance. They were often mistaken for guests. However, an experienced eye could detect that our Swiss were too polite to be guests.

Cultured Commission Merchants

A college of waiters may seem peculiar until you realize how many of your own meals have been ruined by bad service. Although there may have been no cheer leaders in this college, I have no doubt that many of its athletic heroes earned their varsity letters by dropkicking a soup tureen over the goal posts from the forty-five-yard line. Or can you picture another athlete throwing a hard-boiled egg on a dead line from deep center field to the home plate? However, they were all schooled in the science of waiting, knew what to do with their hands, and no patron of Rector's ever was forced to order a glass of water with the thumb on the outside.

When I say our men were salesmen, I mean that they got a percentage on foods which a guest might not think of ordering, such as olives, celery, and *petits fours*. The waiter's bit was 10 per cent., which would amount to from thirty to sixty dollars a month. In addition to this, he received twenty-five cents for pint champagne corks and fifty cents for the corks from quart bottles. This was paid to him by rival wine agents, seeking to increase the sale of their beverages. That would run into another thirty to sixty dollars a month. Of course, we never allowed our waiters to suggest any particular brand of wine, as there was too much danger of angering the other dealers. But I have no doubt that some waiters were subsidized by unethical agents. In spite of the fact that the pay was less than a dollar a day, a good waiter could clean up $1,000 a month in legitimate service.

We employed sixty waiters and twenty omnibuses. The day men came in at ten in the morning and worked until two, and took a three-hour recess in the afternoon. They then came back and worked until after the supper rush at two in the morning. The night men came on at ten in the evening and worked straight through until closing.

There were eight captains of waiters who all retired rich on a pay of seventy-five dollars a month. Three cashiers were necessary to keep tabs on the business and five checkers to check and add up on the food service. The cashiers also waited on the cigar stand and were under the direction of a head cigar man, who had charge of a humidor which always carried a stock of the finest Cuban cigars. We would not surrender our cigar stand to the ubiquitous concessionaire, as my father refused to consider profits when compared with the risk of a patron getting a bad after-dinner smoke. Our cigar man went to Cuba every winter to select the various brands of leaf and our humidor never moistened less than $20,000 worth of tobacco. This man was paid fifty dollars a week—a huge pay in those days of wagon picnics and raglan overcoats.

He even drew down larger pay than the maître d'hôtel, who was the most important man in the establishment, but received only $150 a month. Our maître d'hôtel was Paul Perret, and we lured him from Delmonico's with honeyed words and promises of a better life to come, and he more than repaid us in service and good will. He knew everybody in the world and could address almost any man in his native tongue. He had an uncanny gift of guessing a patron's nationality by appearance alone.

The next man to him in personal value was our manager, Andrew Mehler, another importation from the Italian-Swiss canton in the Alps. We trapped him also in our happy hunting grounds in Delmonico's after he had been with them more than twenty-nine years. We baited him with an offer of $10,000 a year and double that amount in stock. He was an excellent man, a good greeter, and knew his business from A to Izzard. He drew a large salary because he received absolutely no tips, while Perret's poor wages were more than compensated by the fact that his job was worth $25,000 a year in tips and bonuses.

Under Royal Protection

The real salaries started with Mehler. In fact, he got the only big salary in the dining room. It was vastly different downstairs, where men were cooks. Our chef was Emil

Hederer, who landed in Rector's en route from Alsace-Lorraine via the old Bellevue in Philadelphia. George Boldt brought Emil to New York when he opened the Waldorf-Astoria and we snared him by dangling $7,000 a year under his capable nose. He was a man well over sixty, heavy set, a big eater and drinker. The high spot in his career was when his great specialty, terrapin à la Maryland, found its way into Buckingham Palace during the reign of Queen Victoria. Boldt sent Emil's finest effort all the way from the Bellevue in Philadelphia to England.

Emil received an autographed photograph of the Queen, which he carried next to his heart and exhibited at every chance. He finally lost it during a dispute with a Sixth Avenue car conductor over the paying of a five-cent fare. When the conductor pointed an indignant finger at the fare register, Emil pulled out the picture of Victoria and waved it under his chin. The last wave carried it out of the window and it was never found. He was a staunch Frenchman and often retarded service by quarrelling with the night chef, a stalwart German from the other side of the Rhine. Their arguments were the joy of downstairs. Emil hated whistling in his kitchen and often chased musical bus boys upstairs with a knife. The only time he ever condoned whistling was when an impish bus boy paraded past the night chef, whose name was Ritter, whistling The Marseillaise.

Ritter's ears stiffened when he heard the national anthem of France and he grabbed the boy by the neck. Emil, who had hated whistling up to this minute, came to the lad's rescue and, in turn, grabbed Ritter by the neck.

Ritter said, "That boy can't whistle in my kitchen," meaning, of course, that the boy couldn't whistle The Marseillaise.

Emil said, "He can whistle anything he wants," putting the seal of approval on any whistled aria—provided it was The Marseillaise.

I heard the uproar and came downstairs to learn the trouble and straighten it out, sending the bus boy upstairs with a delayed order. Five minutes later the boy strolled through the kitchens whistling The Watch on the Rhine. Emil made a rush for him, and the same argument ensued when Ritter came to his defense. While Emil and Ritter were rolling over the floor in deadly combat, with Emil shouting, "He can't whistle in my kitchen," and Ritter roaring, "He can whistle all he wants," the boy went past their entangled bodies whistling Yankee Doodle.

However, he made the mistake of continuing his whistling into the main dining room, and he was discreetly booted downstairs by a suave captain, landing on both Emil and Ritter, who stopped their quarrel long enough to give him a good international spanking. I never knew that boy's name but have no doubt that he is a great comedian on the stage to-day. Talent like that is wasted in a kitchen.

Chapter 8

An Ante-Prohibition Bartender

Chefs are as temperamental as pianists or opera singers. All our trouble was downstairs in the kitchen. The cooks were as jealous of one another as the family cat is when the first faint whimper of a new baby is heard in the household. Emil became too difficult to handle and we had to let him go. Next to Emil in importance was Charles Perraudin, chief sauce cook, from the Province of Touraine. He was a young fellow of twenty-eight when we made our drive on Delmonico's and got him for $5,000 a year, with a bonus of $2,000. When Emil left, he became head chef.

It is Perraudin who must receive credit for the wonderful Rector cuisine. He was with us from start to finish and his head contained the food wisdom of the ages. He left Rector's to enlist in the French Army in 1914, was gassed, and is now engaged in the automobile-accessory business in Switzerland. He was young, active, and tireless, and was the keystone of our business. In addition to being responsible for the cuisine, he was overseer of seventeen roast cooks, fry cooks, and the *garde manger,* or cold meats and salads room. Two firemen, four vegetable cooks, and four porters also were under his direction.

This about completed our establishment, with the exception of the bar. The head bartender was Johnny Graus, a product of the Chicago school of mixing and pouring. He was one of the best-known bartenders in America and had three bartenders under him. One of these bartender's sole duty was to squeeze orange juice for Diamond Jim Brady. He worked harder than any of the others. I don't know what he is doing now, but he is the only bartender I ever knew who cannot be arrested for sticking to his original trade.

There is still one important servant not yet mentioned. He was on the payroll for only fifty a month, yet to-day he is better off financially than anybody connected with Rector's. He never came into the restaurant. All I remember of him is that his name was John. He was the carriage starter and never missed a night in fifteen years. To-day he is the owner of numerous apartment buildings in New York City. He was John to me, John to all our patrons, and I have still to learn his last name.

John's recipe for success was a huge Irish smile. When he grinned a welcome to a carriage party, his lips stretched an octave over a keyboard of the whitest teeth I have ever seen. He also knew everybody by name and made it a point to learn our patrons' home addresses. When a patron called a cabby and said, "Home, Jasper," it was up to John to dish up the correct house number and street. He never failed. After quitting the restaurant game, I lived for three years in a fine Riverside Drive apartment. My landlord was my former doorman.

Dainty Morsels at Secondhand

As dishwashers are active participants in all restaurant service, we must add six expert dish scourers and six capable cleaners of glassware. This completes the whole personnel of Rector's, making a total of almost 150 servants for an establishment seating only 500 diners. I might add that the dishwashing is a concession in the best cafés of Paris.

While we pay our china scrubbers very good wages, the French concessionaires bid eagerly for the honor of wiping Parisian plates. Their contracts entitle them to all the food remaining on the dish. They gather this up, sort it into pretty little packages and resell it over the counter of a *petite charcuterie.*

The secondhand food is much prized by the working people in the environs of Paris, and many a poor man has put the *coup de grâce* to a turkey wing which was slightly wounded the night before by the teeth of a duke or a princess. There is nothing wasted in France, and there is no better illustration than the *pot-au-feu,* meaning the pot on the fire. The wood is always burning on this altar of thriftiness and the soup is eternally simmering. All scraps and bones are thrown into the *pot-au-feu*. Our old Greenwich Village friend, the dunker, is the deadly enemy of the *pot-au-feu,* because he sops up everything with his vigilant crust of bread and leaves nothing to be tossed into the caldron of economy.

Americans can learn a lesson from the pot on the fire, for Europe could exist on what we throw away. Our enormous waste at banquets alone would feed a nation. I recall the dinner given to Prince Henry of Prussia on his visit here early in the century. It made one of Nero's festivals resemble a hobo's hand-out on a window sill. When Prince Henry came to America he was given a tremendous welcome. It was the whole-hearted greeting which furnished the Kaiser with the befuddled impression that he could rely on America's neutrality some few years later.

Henry was the sailor prince of the Hohenzollerns. He came into Rector's very informally on several occasions. We also entertained several of the Kaiser's sons when they were travelling incognito in this country later on. Very few people knew of this visit of Wilhelm's youngsters. I think their names were Adelbert, Egbert, or some other kind of berts and eggs. The dinner given to Prince Henry was tendered at the Waldorf and was directed by the famous Oscar. This illustrious juggler of pots and pans was another individual who seemed to have no surname. He went through life on the name of Oscar, like a buggy on one wheel.

I will give you an impression of the tremendous eating and drinking at this dinner by mentioning the wine service alone. It started off with 150 bottles of amontillado sherry from Spain, valued at four dollars a bottle. There followed a salvo from a battery of 350 bottles of Rhine wine and the same amount of sauternes. One is a French white wine and the other is a German white wine, to be served with the fish course. You could figure these wines around four dollars a bottle. Then 750 slim decanters of Bordeaux red claret washed down the entrée, with the assistance of a like number of Burgundy carafes.

So far the drinking was merely summer lightning. The storm broke after the entrée, when 3,000 bottles of champagne thundered a greeting to the royal guest. About this time the conversation began to get thin, but the talk was thick. The champagne averaged four dollars a quart. The famous Fine Champagne Cognac of the vintage of 1811 was served with the coffee. This ancient nectar cost twenty dollars a bottle.

There was plenty of speech making at that dinner. The talking started with one guest speaking at a time, but all 1,500 were orating together at the finish. These very damp statistics were furnished to me by William La Hiff, now a prominent restaurateur in New York, but then a bartender at the Waldorf. Tommy Hilliard was the manager of the hotel at that time. He was the most efficient man in the hotel business in America. He was also the strictest.

It was Hilliard's strictness which enabled him to become the biggest figure in the hotel game after a humble start as yardman at the Bellevue, Philadelphia. A yardman is the man who carries the cans of debris from the kitchen to the wagon.

This was probably the biggest dinner ever held indoors in this country. I have heard of enormous barbecues in the West, but these were nothing to compare with the pink tea tendered Prince Henry of Prussia.

And When the Pie was Opened

Rector's never got the big dinners because of our limited seating capacity. We served many banquets to prominent men and women, but none which equaled the famous—or rather, notorious—Seeley dinner at Sherry's. It was at this dinner that Little Egypt, the hootchy-kootchy dancer, was served in a pie. She was very flimsily clad and the dinner was raided by Peaches Chapman, the famous police captain of the Tenderloin.

The Tenderloin was a district north of Thirtieth Street and west of Broadway. It derived its name from the fact that police eating in restaurants south of Thirtieth Street were served rump steaks and cow meat. When they were transferred north of Thirtieth, the meats were much better. They got tenderloin steaks from the prime steers. Therefore the Tenderloin district owes its name to the police themselves. When Peaches raided Sherry's, he was a little off his beat. He did not belong at that dinner, but neither did Little Egypt.

This dinner gave a lot of publicity to Sherry's. Every newspaper in the land carried a front-page description of the affair and it was cabled all over the world. This publicity was very distasteful to Mr. Sherry, who had no idea that Little Egypt was going to be smuggled across the borders of exclusive society in a deep-dish pie like a Chinaman crossing the Mexican border in the middle of a flock of sheep. The agitation over the girl in the pie was long and furious. Late Victorian modesty had been outraged.

As I said in a previous chapter, there was never any scandal connected with Rector's. The closest we came to it was when a gambler and bookmaker dined in our place one evening and was shot shortly afterward in a two-wheeler cab. His companion was a beautiful actress. She was acquitted. The only strange feature about the case was that the actress was not one of the original Floradora Sextet.

Rector's figured very largely on the stage. Nat Wills' great song hit in the earliest of Flo Ziegfeld's Follies was If a Table in Rector's Could Talk. Nat married a great circus bareback rider. She was a wondrous picture as she pirouetted around the spangled ring on a milk-white steed, now turning a double somersault and now leaping through a paper hoop like an elephant crashing through a bass drum. She was a very big woman and I often marveled at her grace. Their married life was yes and no. That is, like many other marriages, it had its quarrels.

Lew Dockstader once told me that he heard the sounds of a family quarrel emanating from the wife's dressing room and soon Nat came hurtling through the air, to land with a tremendous thump on the floor outside. As Lew went over to help him to his feet, Nat sat there with his head in his hands muttering, "I should have married the horse." The remarkable part of the proceeding was that Dockstader swears that Nat was thrown through the door without the door first having been opened, but the story is probably apocryphal.

The Barber-Shop Blues

Lew Dockstader was the last of the old-time minstrels. He went into vaudeville when minstrelsy faded from the American stage and became a great monologist, sharing honors with Nat Wills, Fred Niblo, Charley Case, Ezra Kendall, and Jim Thornton. Thornton was the author of that beautiful ballad, When You Were Sweet Sixteen. He was a regular patron of Rector's. His monologue has never been surpassed for humor and could still be used to-day after thirty years. He used to tell about going into a barber shop, saying that he was the man who first discovered that the barber used your ear for a mug to mix his lather. In his own words: "He put a hot towel on my face and scalded me alive. When I asked him why he put such a hot towel on my face, he explained that it was too hot to hold in his bare hands. Then a little boy about five years of age climbed on a soap box and started to shave me. He started to cut my face into jigsaw puzzles. When I objected to a boy shaving me, his father told me it was the lad's birthday and we had to let him do anything he wanted to on his birthday. All this time a dog was running around the chair howling and barking. When I asked the man why the dog was running around the chair, he told me that the dog had got a piece of ear that morning and wouldn't go away until he got another."

Charley Case was very nervous. He overcame this by twisting a piece of string around his finger while talking to his audience. He used to talk about his family. He explained that they lived next door to the county jail, because Mother was sentimental and wanted to be just as close to Father as she could get. Father was apparently a very brave man, because he used to hunt lions. One day he caught up to a lion, but decided not to shoot it. This wasn't because he had lost his nerve, but because he was afraid that it might be a neighbor's lion.

Dockstader was the first monologist to specialize in topics of the day. No matter what subject was agitating the newspapers and the public, Lew always bobbed up with an appropriate jest. When Colonel Roosevelt was running for President, Lew made up to represent Teddy and the resemblance was startling. He used to stroll out on the stage with a big stick, which never failed to get a roar of laughter. When Colonel Roosevelt became involved in a political controversy with another colonel—let's say it was Colonel Blotto—Lew summarized the situation thus: "When they speak of Roosevelt as a kernel they mean a soldier. When they speak of Blotto as a kernel they mean the inside of a nut."

The monologist has the most difficult role on the stage. Without music, scenery, or foils, he must hold his audience by his personality alone. Nat Wills had the strongest voice I ever heard on the stage. His trump card was the singing—or rather, bellowing—of parodies on popular songs of the day. He also used to recite fictitious telegrams. Here are samples of them, and they never failed to get uproarious laughter. First, he would read: "Twentieth Century Limited four hours late. Reason—it struck a cow." He would pause a second and then continue: "Erie Express on time. Reason—unknown."

Another famous monologist of this time was the Man with the Green Gloves who read supposed epitaphs in a manner to excite tremendous outbursts of laughter. I never knew just what was funny about an inscription on a tombstone, but here is one that caused old-time audiences to shriek with glee: "The Hudson River is wide and deep, but not a very elegant place to sleep." The Man with the Green Gloves was James Richmond Glenroy, but I never did discover who was the Girl with the Auburn Hair. The Girl with the Auburn Hair was a beautiful creature who sang The Holy City in a magnificent voice. Her identity is still a mystery to the millions who enjoyed her singing.

Not the least of the monologists who frequented Rector's was Marshall P. Wilder, whose face was the most elastic I have ever seen. He actually had a thousand different expressions chasing one another across his features. His success was the more remarkable because he was a cripple from birth, and also a dwarf. You forgot his infirmities the instant you looked at his face.

A Fashionable Ringside

While others were forced to pay to see theatrical stars, the theatrical headliners paid to see Rector's. Dramatists, producers, and actors all gathered there from eleven until closing, which was usually about three. Grouped around one table would be Clyde Fitch, Richard Harding Davis, Charles Dillingham, Alfred Henry Lewis, Jack London, Henry Blossom, Charles Frohman, and Otis Skinner.

At another table would be David Graham Phillips, who was shot down by a maniac coming out of the Princeton Club in Gramercy Park shortly before his story *The Grain of Dust* was published serially in the *Saturday Evening Post*. It was one of the most interesting serials I have ever read. I remember the heroine was the forerunner of the modern flapper, for she had the pleasing habit of sprinkling perfume on lump sugar and eating it.

At Phillips's table would be Harry Lauder and his American manager, William Morris. Next to them would be Victor Herbert. Of all the prominent folk who patronized Rector's, the most appreciative, the heartiest, most democratic, and most sincere was Victor Herbert. He loved to entertain his friends. The minute he stepped inside the door our orchestra swung into one of his many musical hits. He never failed to thank them for their courtesy. They loved him, as did everyone else.

Weber and Fields, McIntyre and Heath, Montgomery and Stone, Jack Norworth and Nora Bayes were four famous teams who often clustered around one table. Mayor Gaynor often dropped in with his very good friend, Ira Leo Bamberger, an attorney. Gaynor enjoyed good music, art, and drama. I remember a friend introducing Ira Leo

Bamberger to Henry E. Dixey, then starring in *Adonis* under the direction of Edward E. Rice, who also put on the famous extravaganza *"1492."* The friend said, "Mr. Dixey, I want you to meet Ira Leo Bamberger."

Dixey said, "I didn't catch all those names."

The friend repeated, "Ira Leo Bamberger."

"Oh, yes," replied Dixey; "three nice boys."

It was rarely that good humor turned to rancor. We had some fights in the restaurant and they all received immense publicity, not because of the excellence of the fisticuffs but because of the prominence of the combatants. Charles Hawtrey, playing in *A Message from Mars,* once challenged his fellow player, Arthur Playfair, and the two fought it out. The argument started over a rarebit and Playfair won the combat.

One of the best fights in Rector's was won by Fred Stone from a collegiate champion hammer thrower, baseball and football star.

Stone was sitting quietly at a table with Rex Beach, Dave Montgomery, Maxey Blumenthal, and Sam Elsass. There were only two parties in the place, as it was after closing time. Both parties arose at the same time and went out to get their hats. Beach had a very peculiar floppy cap and the collegian made some remark about it. Rex paid no attention, but real trouble started when Dave Montgomery started to go through the revolving door and the big collegian gave him assistance in the shape of a shove which landed Dave in the middle of the street.

The next to enter the revolving door was Fred Stone, and the stalwart line plunger wanted to do the same thing to Fred. Stone advised the youth to keep his hands off the door, whereupon the enthusiastic collegian grabbed him and started to employ him in the creating of a new intercollegiate record for hammer throwing. Stone whipped over a left hook that landed on the strong man's chin and followed with a right cross that actually struck sparks. By this time the big boy realized that he was in a fight and swung both hands at Fred, who sidestepped and won the championship of Rector's with another right-hander which landed flush on the chin. It wasn't an actual knock-out, but it seemed to take all the battle out of the educated pugilist.

FIGHTS STAGED AT RECTOR'S

Stone turned to Blumenthal and said, "What is the matter with me, Maxey? I can't knock this fellow out."

Stone weighed 100 pounds less than his opponent, but boxed every day with James J. Corbett on the roof of the Globe Theatre. He was the finest athlete in the theatre, hard as nails, and thought nothing of catching a nine-inning baseball game on Saturday morning and then playing a matinee and evening performance.

There was also a nice little set-to between Davy Johnson, the gambler, and George Kessler, the wine agent. Johnson was winning when the fight was stopped. This fight started with the friendly pulling of each other's ties at the table. Kessler finally pulled Johnson's tie too hard and almost choked him. Johnson retaliated by switching his pulling from Kessler's necktie to his nose. Thus mighty oaks from little acorns grow.

Many of the fights were the result of an over-indulgence in wine, except in the case of Fred Stone, who never drank. However, in those days men fought with their fists. It seems to be different now. The bootleggers seem to mix some fierce concoction of boiler compound and TNT which causes men to rush forth and devastate the surrounding hamlets and farm lands. But when it came to getting high prices for our liquor we old restaurateurs had it all over the modern pirate. We would buy our straight rye whisky out of government bonded warehouses at proof. Then to reduce that to the bead, which was at ninety-two proof, we used French spirits and distilled water, fixing the proofage with a hydrometer. When reduced to the bead, this whisky would stand us, less the discounts, about two dollars a gallon. We charged forty cents a drink and there were twenty drinks to a quart and 100 to a gallon. We therefore received forty dollars a gallon, a profit of thirty-eight dollars—which proves that the liquor industry was always bootlegging. The present prosperity of the small family, the luxury of owning pianos, radios, phonographs, bungalows, and motor cars is evidence that the American workingman is spending his money in happier and wiser channels. The corner saloon was a cancer eating into the heart of its neighborhood, and I always noticed that the poorer the district, the flashier the saloon.

At the rate of thirty-eight dollars' profit a gallon we actually made more than $2,000 clear gain on a barrel of whisky. There is a mark for bootleggers to shoot at. And if we had followed the present custom of diluting the stuff until one bottle becomes the mother of two other bottles, then we would have made $6,000 a barrel. But I want to make it clear that Rector's was not a bar-room.

We specialized on our foods and I am quoting alcoholic algebra to show that the unknown quantity was another X in the saloonkeeper's cash register. Of the thousands of our patrons, I cannot say that one was a drunkard. They were all men and women of brains and ability. The toper of that day is the same idiot of the present who drinks paints, oil, and varnishes. The only difference is that the booze of to-day is so poisonous that one drop of it is powerful enough to nickel-plate an iceberg.

Of course, on the old-fashioned New Year's Eve, your ancestors considered it their duty to home, mother, and country to drink the New Year in and themselves out, and they performed this obligation very thoroughly. They thought the way to start the New Year right was with a headache. New Year's Eve and election nights were riotous evenings in the old times. Of the two, I consider election night the noisier. Republicans would celebrate because their candidate was victorious and Democrats would carouse because their man was defeated. No matter who won or lost, everybody joined in the festivities. On these nights we locked our doors and admission was by card only. We boarded up our big windows with heavy planks because of the tremendous crowds surging on the sidewalks.

Demand for tables at Rector's on these nights was so great that we could have used Madison Square Garden as an annex for our overflow and filled it.

Although there was no dancing in our place at that time, the crowd amused itself. Eva Tanguay, Blanche Ring, and Lillian Russell would oblige with songs, even though the ladies had not yet achieved a vote at that period. Not to be outdone by the ladies, William Pruette would rumble, "I want what I want when I want it," his famous success from Herbert's opera *Mlle. Modiste* in a basso profundo which rattled Rector's to its foundation. Some 500 diners would join in the chorus, accentuating each "want" with a bang of the fist on the table.

But, as usual, the smallest man made the biggest noise, for Tod Sloan, who was just back from riding Lord Beresford's horses to victory in England, always placed a nice bonnet on the climax by shooting off a small brass cannon on the roof of our restaurant. Tod employed a stalwart valet to carry the cannon around on state occasions. The morning Tod and Julia Sanderson ate their wedding breakfast at Rector's, Tod actually shot the cannon off in the dining room as a salute to his new bride.

To those who desire to be the life of the party, but who can neither sing, dance, nor do feats of legerdemain, I suggest a fifty-pound brass cannon and plenty of ammunition. If properly used, you can shoot your way into the social swim—provided it doesn't first blow you out of the tank.

Chapter 9

Good Linen Dies Young

The younger generation has small respect for decrepit institutions of the past. I don't blame them. I felt the same way myself when I was young. However, I can inform the Channel swimmers and handicap golfers of to-day that their fathers and mothers visited New York with two places of interest in view. One was Grant's Tomb and the other was Rector's. We had the liveliest institution then, but I think Grant has the edge on us now. I have no doubt that we served wedding breakfasts to these same fathers and mothers. Anyway, there were many shy young couples with brand-new shoes who walked bravely into Rector's around 1900 and sought to order chicken à la King with the metropolitan *savoir-faire*. Had they chosen any curried dish, we could easily have shaken the necessary rice from his lapels and her bonnet.

I want to say that no young married couple ever fooled me. We could spot them a mile away in a heavy fog. If we had any doubt about it, this was removed when our orchestra played the Wedding March from Lohengrin. The victims were the ones who blushed. We were extra nice to these young folks and tried to make them feel at home in a strange city. Of course, wedding marches meant nothing to old campaigners embarking on their fourth and fifth marriages. Whenever Nat Goodwin or DeWolf Hopper walked in with another bride, our musicians always played The Minstrel Boy to the War Has Gone.

We never objected when the young bride shyly smuggled a monogrammed doily inside her waist as a souvenir of her wedding breakfast in our place. But we did protest when an experienced divorcee or a veteran debutante tried sleight-of-hand tricks with our silverware and expensive table linen. But in spite of our best efforts, our linen evaporated very rapidly. We started in 1899 with $30,000 worth of linen imported from the north of Ireland. Inside of a year we were forced to place another order with the same Belfast firm for another $10,000 worth of linen. Some of our first shipment was decorating tables in homes, but most of it had succumbed to the wear and tear of everyday use and repeated trips to the laundry.

Linen is an important accessory in a well-ordered café. There is a pleasant feel to good linen. It is cool to the touch. It adds richness to the appearance of the table and an additional luster to the silver and crystal service. Nondescript cotton and shoddy cloths should be avoided at all times. A guest rising from a dining table covered with cotton cloth looks as if he had been chased through an orchard of fuzzy confetti. His coat is smeared with clinging lint, which is very annoying. There are many tests of good linen, but the oldest and the best is the one used by our grandmothers. Wet the tip of the finger and apply it to the cloth. If the cloth wets all the way through, quickly, it is good linen. Cotton has a nap which acts as a blotter and absorbs the moisture before it reaches the cloth. Linen has no rough nap.

We lost our entire shipment of linen for many reasons. First, the napkins and doilies were easy to fold and carry away. Second, repeated visits to the laundry. Third, careless smokers placed their cigars on the table and burned holes through the cloth, the table top, the felt pad, and right into the table itself. Fourth, the stains from red wine were impossible to remove unless attended to immediately. Fifth, the diners kept books on the cloth with pen and ink or indelible pencil. There are four pieces in the linen family. Doily, napkin, table top, and tablecloth. Our first shipment included 6,000 napkins, 4,000 doilies, 1,000 tablecloths, and the same number of tops. A top is a square piece of linen placed over the cloth to freshen up the table. It saves changing the entire cloth, which is irritating to diners. Our napkins were full twenty-eight inches square. A man with one under his chin looked as if he were wearing an old-fashioned nightgown.

Very hot plates and chafing dishes also eliminated many fine cloths from the tournament. The little prairie fires on rum omelets often overran the silver platter and streaked a scorched detour across the linen. Our losses would be much greater to-day. We bought fine linen cloths for five dollars in 1900 which would cost fifteen dollars apiece at present prices.

The Rector griffin was embroidered on every piece of linen. It was also etched in every piece of glass in the crystal service and engraved on the silver. The silver service set us back about $40,000. It included many different shapes and sizes of spoons, forks, and knives. I shall not bother you with details other than to say that there are few stores which carry a retail stock as complete and as large as Rector's table equipment. We tried to keep our establishment fresh and cheerful, and we succeeded all the year round, with the usual exceptions. These two exceptions were Thanksgiving Day and Christmas Eve.

The Lonesomest Day in the Year

I have never seen anything more mournful than a man dining in a restaurant on these two great home holidays. He is the most forlorn individual in the world. He either has no home or he is far away from his family. Of course, there were many New Yorkers who considered Rector's their home, but it was a doleful substitute for a home on Christmas Eve. Thanksgiving Day was not so bad, but the Yuletide affected our entire organization. The waiters were dreaming of the far Alps, and the Russian orchestra played weird selections which should be strummed only under the light of the pale northern stars. We never had more than two or three parties on these nights. In one alcove there would be two or three men with their elbows on the tables and their heads in their hands. Over in the corner, a girl crying.

Never be envious of a man dining in an exclusive restaurant or club on Christmas Eve—provided your footprints in the snow are in the direction of a home. The only way we could cheer ourselves up on this night was to send a waiter out on Broadway with instructions to pick up a dozen hobos, the raggeder the better. We sat them at a big table and fed them turkey, cranberry sauce, and plum pudding until we took the wrinkles out of their stomachs. A good cigar over black coffee would transform them into the jolliest guests of the year. The solemn regulars in the corner of the room would perk up and order a round of drinks for the tattered vagrants. The girl in the corner would stop crying and send over a box of candy. We started this custom in Chicago and kept it up until we closed in New York. We never lost a piece of silver to one of these stray guests.

It was different on New Year's Eve, when reservations were at a premium. Our receipts for this one night were always more than $10,000. Saturday nights and other holidays netted us around $5,000. The average business for the rest of the year was about $2,000 a day. These are enormous sums when you realize that we are speaking of twenty-five years ago, when a patron could dine well in

Rector's for $1.25 à la carte. We served no table d'hôte. The same sum would also get you excellent food and service in Delmonico's and Sherry's. A man was a big citizen who spent twenty dollars an evening in entertaining four dinner guests in those days. To-day this sum would hardly enable you to complete a cycle in a Cathay cafeteria.

Steak à la Fifteen Minutes

The man who spent twenty dollars a night for a party of five would be able to include two bottles of champagne and a round of cigars. If he had taken his guests to the theatre, he would have expended an additional seven dollars and fifty cents.

Contrast this almost Colonial evening with to-day. Say, the afternoon that Papyrus thought he was racing Zev. You started out for the track with your girl and found that the minimum price to see the English horse chase his rival around the curves was $5.50. That's eleven for two. The Follies had their *première* that same evening and orchestra seats were selling for twenty-two dollars, which is just a score of degrees above the boiling point, Fahrenheit.

After the show, your lady was eager to attend the opening of a new night club where table reservations were only eleven dollars a cover, which included food, but not liquids. Your total for two up to this minute was seventy-seven dollars. The longer you stayed in this establishment the larger grew your expense parchment—a slip of paper known to travelling salesmen as the swindle sheet. A bottle of ginger ale cost you nothing less than a dollar in this night club.

No wonder that Bert Kelmar, after an evening in there with his wife and seven relatives, beckoned to a waiter and said, "Hey, waiter, bring me the check and a fright wig."

To those not in the theatrical game, I will explain that a fright wig is a toupee on which the hair is made to stand on end by the yanking of a cord which runs down back of the neck and through the sleeve. The fright wig is funny on the stage, but not quite so humorous in a restaurant. My own hair has often stood up on its own merits after I have scanned the check in a New York night club. The difference between Rector's checks and the additions of to-day is that we actually stuck to simple adding, while all they know now is multiplication.

The $1.25 Rector meal would include any entrée you desired, although our clientele did not have that robust Rocky Mountain appetite which yelled for beef on the hoof. Our patrons went in for dainty dishes, such as sea food, poultry, and game. We did not serve many beef sirloins, although Rector's was responsible for that very popular and well-known dish, the steak à la minute. After waiting an hour or so for this order to be served, you might naturally wonder how it ever got its maiden name of à la minute. It was the swiftest steak we served, because it was sliced thin as a wafer and cooked very quickly. If timed by reliable handicappers, I think the best we could have claimed for it was steak à la fifteen minutes.

Some guests pronounced minute with the accent on the last syllable, which made it mean very small or even infinitesimal. These guests were closer to the truth. But I refuse to validate that old story about the guest who asked his waiter to point out his steak and was informed that it was hiding under a pea. We were never fortunate enough to get peas of that size. That would be almost as bad as the café which served its food on cracked dishes, with the entire meal in the crack.

If we knew where to procure a pea like that we would have included it in our *carte du jour,* as we imported ripe figs from Arabia, winter peaches from Africa, and the alligator pear from the tropics. Napoleon said that an army moves on its stomach, but we appealed to our army's palate. We fed about 1,000 people a day for an average of two dollars a patron. Some 200 of these were luncheon customers who nibbled very tidily for thirty-five, forty, and fifty cents. The other 800 were made of sterner stuff and consumed two barrels of oysters a day, four gallons of olives, 500 lobsters, ten dozen chickens, the same number of squabs, as much pastry as you could pack on a hay scale, and a fair day's bag of canvasback, grouse, woodcock, pheasant, and quail. Once again, I must deny that we sold enough oyster stew to float the United States Navy and that the Navy could sail around in that stew for a year without striking an oyster.

A Giant Bouquet of Greens

You can also add ten gallons of crab meat and about 400 fillets of sole. We did not buy the entire crab. It was shipped from Chesapeake Bay in gallon tins. After being caught, the crab was boiled and then tapped with a small hammer until two large flakes of crab meat dropped out of the shell. These flakes were consigned to Rector's without having been touched by a human hand. The rest of the crab was sold as seconds. The daily bouquet of greens averaged about 1,000 heads of lettuce, endives, romaine, and celery. This would have made a nice *boutonnière* for Og, King of Bashan, who tore up mountains by the roots.

I almost forgot that stream-line pearl of the farm, the egg. Starting in Lewiston on the Niagara in 1825 with a small order of ham and eggs served to a French-Canadian trapper, the Rectors gradually increased their egg power until we were breaking thousands a day to be utilized as the base of sauces and pastry. When we reached Broadway, we still continued to smile upon the egg, but we frowned upon its poor relation, the ham. Like many successful men who had climbed the ladder of success, we kicked out the rungs beneath us. We allowed no ham and eggs to be served during the dinner hour. The Welsh rabbit also was barred during the supper service, and so was that last gasp of the dying gladiator, the club sandwich.

Personally I like all three; but we were ever striving to increase the aura of exclusiveness emanating from Rector's, so we were forced to drop three faithful favorites into the Bosporus. However, if you could order des *oeufs au jambon,* you would get a mysterious order which would prove to be ham and eggs when translated into English. A slight dash of hypocrisy is the alloy which strengthens sincerity. But let a man order ham and eggs by their correct labels, and we blanketed him with the chill of the Alaskan night.

However, you could eat ham and eggs until your ankles groaned under the excess baggage, provided you did so after theatre hours. Then the restaurant was yours to do unto as you could afford. Our embargo on the three dishes mentioned was due to the fact that a man eating a Welsh rabbit, ham and eggs, or a club sandwich never ordered anything else. His meal was usually bracketed by his imagination. I know not what food Alexander ate that men called him great, but it could not have included these three superb creations of a moron's dull moment.

The Chef's Favorite Perfume

Another rap against the Welsh rabbit was, like a fat man's snoring in a sleeping car, its presence must be shared by everybody in the vicinity. It is impossible to confine the aromatic effulgence of a Welsh rabbit to one table. It radiates its toasted rays throughout the room. The same is true of corned beef and cabbage, which, if cooked in our kitchens, might have affected the aristocratic fragrance of the casserole specialties. I say this, knowing that ham and eggs and corned beef and cabbage finished first and second in a recent culinary beauty contest. I was one man who voted for them.

But our French chefs would no more have thought of cooking corned beef and cabbage than Tiffany would have dreamed of selling building material. The art of French cooking seems to be to destroy the original flavor of the food and substitute a chef's idea of what the dish should be. It is possible to paint a lily, but you cannot enamel a cabbage.

However, different lands, different customs. I could never understand the chef's hatred of cabbage and his strong admiration for that hardy, bulbous, ever-blooming rosebud of the onion family, the garlic. I will say that garlic never actually appeared in the food. That would be a *faux pas*. It was a hidden jewel, doomed to blush unseen, but not to waste its fragrance on the desert air. He rubbed it on the steaks, rubbed it on the chickens, and rubbed it on the lamb. He rubbed it on the pots and pans in which he prepared ragouts and stews. I remonstrated with him, but he continued to rub the meats with it. He held the small button of garlic between his thumb and forefinger and rubbed with the intense thoughtfulness of a man seeking to erase the mistakes of Nature by slow, rhythmic pressure. My arguments failed to move him and I fled before he rubbed it on me. I often suspected that he rubbed it in his tub before taking a bath. Doctors now say that garlic has great curative powers, and they are right. Garlic cured me—of garlic.

Before taking you out of the kitchens, I would like to give you a recipe which was the last will and testament of many thousands of eggs during the reign of the Rector dynasty. This recipe is for stuffed eggs à la Rector:

> Boil four eggs until they become hard. Remove shells and allow eggs to cool. Slice in halves,

lengthwise. Remove the yolks and force them through a very fine sieve. Add to the yolks an equal amount of *pâté de foie gras*. Mix well together. Then press the mixture back into the eggs and place eggs in a deep silver or glass platter. Spread over a liberal amount of sauce Mornay. [I gave you the recipe for sauce Mornay in a previous chapter.] Place under grill and allow the sauce to come to a rich golden brown. Serve from the platter directly to the dish.

When prepared rightly, this is a dish to snatch away from a king. It is most appetizing and not difficult to prepare. It is a little heavy for afternoon tea, but makes a beautiful bridge-whist luncheon, especially if the cards have been running right. It is also very nice for basket parties in the motor car. But for a picnic in the woods you must leave out the sauce Mornay. Instead, substitute a Russian dressing, which can be carried out in a separate preserve jar and poured over the eggs when ready to eat. Here is a splendid recipe for Russian dressing à la Rector. By this time you may have noticed that, whether the dish be French, Russian, or Mongolian, it is always à la Rector. We always placed this tag at the end of a recipe for the same reason that the little boy put the elephant in the puzzle—to make it more difficult:

> Take two-thirds mayonnaise, one-third chili sauce, the quantity depending on the number of persons in the party. Put in a heaping teaspoonful of chopped green peppers, minced very fine. Also an equal amount of minced olives and the same quantity of shallots. Mix all very well together.

That's your Russian dressing and just about the simplest tune you ever played on your kitchen piano. A shallot is of the onion family, but smaller, and hasn't got the sharp tang of the onion. By this time I am not certain whether I am writing an autobiography or a cookbook. I might mention that these recipes are from a period when there was no dieting, few vegetarians, and no health foods. All food was supposed to be healthful and the ladies ate without thought of the morrow and its extra poundage. It was an eating generation, and though many dug their graves with their teeth, they enjoyed it.

The nearest we had to whole-wheat and gluten breads in those days was a sort of Graham. There were no breakfast foods and cereals. The good old stand-by in American homes was oatmeal, and you could take it or leave it. People ate steaks in the Western mornings and apple pie in the New England dawns. Business men would eat terrific meals around noon and then stagger aimlessly through the rest of their office hours, wondering what had happened to the climate. The age was the renaissance of gout. There was a plethora of heavy meats and a corresponding fulness of ponderous side dishes.

Chapter 10

A Check on the Bad News

The average span of life is ten years longer to-day because of the balanced eating. There has been a tremendous increase in the eating of vegetables and greens. In those days folks didn't go in much for greens. I quote McIntyre, of McIntyre and Heath, in their famous sketch, *The Ham Tree,* as an indication of the general feeling about lettuce, asparagus, and the rest of that family. The two were making their way to Europe by easy stages in a wheelbarrow. Their food had run out and Heath was supplying forage in the shape of watercress, scallions, and dandelions. This diet got to be too much for McIntyre, who finally remonstrated to Heath about their food, and Heath informed him that they were vegetarians until they got to Europe.

McIntyre retorted bitterly, "I don't mind being a vegetarian, but I ain't going to be no weeditarian."

Vegetarians or weeditarians, people should eat plenty of salads. The dressing does not add greatly to its food value, but serves its purpose as a garnishing to the flat, leafy flavor of all heads of salad. The best dressing is the French one advocated by Berry Wall. You should check up on the food you serve yourself as carefully as we tabulated all the food served in Rector's. Our checking system was perfected after many years of trials and failures.

We discovered the successful checking system by accident. It happened in Chicago about the time the cash register was invented. We bought one of the first registers at the suggestion of the maker.

The first machine was a big improvement at our cigar counter and attracted a lot of Illinois attention because of its novelty. It reversed the procedure of a shooting gallery, because you first got your cigar and then the bell rang. It worked so well at the cigar counter that my father suggested that a new machine should be made which would register all individual food sales on a guest's check. Up to this time everything had been more or less haphazard and there was a great amount of leakage due to carelessness.

The manufacturer constructed an improved machine for Rector's which was a revelation in the restaurant industry. Every dish which passed the checker's station was stamped upon the check and registered in the machine. There was never any cash in this cash register, because the check was paid by the waiter to the cashier at another station.

At the end of the business day we would add up the dinner, cigar, and bar checks and compare the result with the total on the machine. It always balanced to a penny.

The Original Yes Man

My father invented this system, now in use all over the world. It saved us thousands of dollars a year, because it absolutely removed all chances of carelessness or dishonesty on the part of employees. It simplified bookkeeping, because, like the manipulation of a donkey engine, the whole mechanism centered in one throttle. It also added to the gayety of nations by cancelling that solemn moment at the end of the meal when the guest cowers under a waiter, who, with pad and pencil poised in air, has the manner of a judge about to deal out a heavy sentence to a culprit.

As the check was added up by the register, the waiter was merely a messenger boy bringing in bad news.

Each check was divided into three parts by perforations. The checker retained one stub, the second stub went to the cashier, and the guest was awarded the third, which acted as a receipt. New York establishments laughed at us when we inaugurated our system in Manhattan, but they soon adopted it. We had a battery of registers in the New York Rector's, three food machines, one bar, and one cigar machine. Downstairs, where food and wine were handled in bulk by the purchasing department, we had two old-fashioned bookkeepers with spectacles, green eye shades, and round shoulders. All transactions downstairs were done by count, weight, measure, and personal inspection.

The subterranean bookkeepers kept their daily balance, which dovetailed in with the registers above. If 150 squabs were sent upstairs to the dining room and there were 200 in stock at the start of the day's business there were naturally fifty left. The registers showed 150 sold, which made the daily inventory easy. That's all the system we used. Its advantage can be discerned when you realize that it gives you a daily percentage of your profits or losses, which is vital information in any man's business.

Machines were of great assistance up to this point. But from then on everything depended on personality, atmosphere, and management. Adding up the check correctly doesn't mean that you are going to retain your patron's good will. As an example to the contrary, we cite Europe's attitude toward our war debt. On one occasion we were informed by an irate diner that he merely intended to buy a meal and not the entire restaurant. We soon discovered that a dollar's worth of fixtures was a smaller amount than a penny's worth of good will.

We had one slogan in Rector's. That motto was: The Guest is Right, Right or Wrong. No waiter was allowed to argue with a patron. The waiter's instructions were to report all complaints immediately to the maître d'hôtel, who hurried to the guest's table and straightened out all difficulties by the simple method of agreeing with the guest. I might say that the maître d'hôtel was the original Yes Man of New York and his job depended on his ability to bob his head in the affirmative like a crow in a cornfield.

Politeness and courtesy were responsible for making Rector's the success it was. Our waiters wore full evening dress with the bifurcated coat tails. They were not allowed to wear eyeglasses or white vests and were compelled to shave cleanly every day. Any man caught wearing that crowning atrocity of haberdashery, the dickey, was suspended for ten days. A dickey is a contraption to take the place of a full-dress shirt and has neither sleeves nor body. It is simply a false front fitting under the vest and usually bulges like a balloon tire.

That Apple-Sauce Joke

That veteran of one-night stands and tank towns, Corse Payton, had the habit of giving waiters a free ticket to his shows in lieu of a cash tip. One afternoon he was out of free paper and wrote the pass on the waiter's dickey. The waiter presented the dickey at the door; it was honored and taken up like a regular ticket. Five minutes later the waiter came flying out of the theatre at the end of a boot. Payton had kicked him out for not having a shirt.

Corse Payton was the creator of the famous ten-twenty-and-thirty-cent stock companies known in the profession by the shorter description of ten-twent-and-thirt. Corse played in his own ten-twent-and-thirt repertoire all over the country. He would tackle any show ever written, from burlesque to the melancholy Dane. He was a fine-looking man, very well groomed, and was fond of making speeches in Rector's. He had the voice of a tragedian, and it was in the voice of a tragedian that Corse stood up in our place one night and announced: "There are good actors and there are bad actors, but I am America's best bad actor."

And it was as America's best bad actor that Corse was known thereafter. He knew the value of publicity and never failed to go after his share. Corse had his stock company up in Boston when Charles Frohman presented Maude Adams in that city as the star of *L'Aiglon*. She made a tremendous success, but the work was very exacting and difficult, especially the two matinees every week. Her doctors advised her to take a rest lest she suffer a breakdown, but Miss Adams refused to quit. But it was agreed that she should conserve her energies by playing only one matinee each week instead of the usual Wednesday and Saturday afternoon performances. Frohman had a huge sign stretched across the front of the theatre reading: "Miss Adams will positively give only one matinee a week."

Corse Payton's theatre was directly opposite. The next day there was a bigger sign on Payton's facade, with this inscription: "Corse Payton will positively give only one matinee a day."

There is an expression sweeping America to-day which I heard Corse Payton use twenty-five years ago. Chauffeurs toss it at traffic policemen, traffic policemen catch it in mid-air and hurl it back, bad boys shout it at truant officers, and good little girls shrill it to their fond parents. Even granny tells it to grandpa and there isn't much doubt that grandpa has mumbled it to the manicurist in the barber shop. That expression is "apple sauce." You possibly have used it yourself without knowing how it originated. It started with Thatcher, Primrose, and West, who had one of the greatest minstrel organizations ever assembled. The expression "apple sauce" means anything that is old, trite, and out-of-date. This was the routine of the apple-sauce gag:

> Thatcher: Mr. Interlocutor, a teacher has twelve pupils and only eleven apples.
> West: Yes, Mr. Tambo, a teacher has twelve pupils and only eleven apples.
> Thatcher: That's right. Now she wants to give each pupil an equal share of the apples without cutting the apples. How does she do it?
> West: Let me see. A teacher has twelve pupils and only eleven apples. She wants to give each pupil an equal share of the apples without applying a knife to the fruit. How does she do it? I must confess my ignorance. How does she do it, Mr. Tambo?
> Thatcher: She made apple sauce.

Thatcher used to get a huge laugh with this joke. Naturally, all the other rival minstrels grabbed it, used it, and finally hammered it into an early grave by too much repetition. Audiences refused to laugh at it any more and it was discarded. So any other joke which is old and no good is also called apple sauce. There is something about this expression which is very satisfying. When a motorcycle cop tells you that he is going to give you a ticket, not knowing that you are the mayor's friend, you tell him, "Apple sauce." When he hands you the ticket, he says, "Apple sauce." When you tell the judge you were going only two miles an hour, the judge hands down a verdict of, "Apple sauce." And when you fork over fifteen dollars and bounce out of the court room, the little birdies in the trees seem to be chirping it. I have never seen anything, outside of a sneak thief's skeleton key, which seemed to fit so many situations.

In a previous chapter I spoke about the personnel of my restaurant—the cooks, the head chefs, the waiters, and the captains. There was one crew I forgot to mention, and this outfit was the band of nighthawks operating the fleet of scooped-out and sea-going hacks. The scooped-out hack was the open Victoria, while the seagoing vehicle was the closed hack, more like a brougham. Like Robin Hood's band, they were a merry bunch of outlaws who trimmed the rich—but failed to donate to the poor. There were fifteen or twenty outside of Rector's every night, rain or shine. Their scale of prices depended on their victim's condition of sobriety and knowledge of geography. Their tactics originated the famous expression "run-around." A man who is giving you the run-around is trying to stall you off by using evasive methods.

A Profitable Side Line

A stranger got into a Rector cab one night and asked to be driven to the Hotel Astor, which had just been built and was directly across the street. The cabby was Gas-House Sam, who sensed that his fare was ignorant of the location of the hotel. So Sam click-clicked to his horse and away they went around the block, passing the hotel at the start and passing it again on the completion of the lap. Sam looped the hotel eleven times before he pulled his steed up on its thin haunches and helped his fare out. The charge was three dollars and the runaround proved that a long ride is costlier than a short walk.

Another famous cabby was Ten-Cent Dan. He got his name because no tip was too small for him to accept. I don't doubt, if one of Ten-Cent Dan's fares had been minus the necessary tip, Ten-Cent would have cheerfully accepted trading stamps. Mississippi also drove a cab and made his stand outside Rector's in the last days of that institution. Mississippi's name will be known to boxing fans all over the country for he was a great colored fighter. He still drives a scooped-out hack along Broadway and wears a low, battered high hat and a linen duster. He has fallen upon lean days, for the horse hack gets little patronage. Two years ago, Mississippi was on foot, but Al Jolson came to his rescue and bought him another horse and cab. Last winter must also have been hard times for the ex-fighter, because he was again on foot and was selling raffle tickets for fifty cents apiece, the proceeds of the raffle to be utilized as a fund to bail out his horse, which was being detained by a heartless stable owner as a pawn against a feed bill of $15.20. The raffle was a success, for Mississippi once again is perched on the box, looking in vain for old customers who will never return.

A Pocketful of Marbles

Bounding Dick, Tenderloin Bill, and Frank the Gyp stopped whipping their horses years ago. I do not know what these men did for a living after the taxicab succeeded the oat burner. One cab driver's specialty was rolling drunks. This meant that he sought inebriated fares, whom he proceeded to drive through the park to a dark spot and then frisk. If the victim howled, the cabby never objected to going direct to a police station and being searched. Nothing was ever found on him and he was always discharged.

But so many complaints were lodged against him by fleece-lined customers who had lost their fleeces that an investigation was made and it was discovered that all his customers were paying for two cabs instead of one. Every time he started for the park with a fare, he was followed by another driver in an empty cab, who would drive by the first cab in the park just in time to be handed the victim's watch and money. After the driver came back from his triumphant trip to the police station, the two would divide the plunder. His last drive was a little longer than he reckoned on, for it landed him up in Sing Sing. His horse got a suspended sentence.

This cabby was a fine actor, for after having been given a clean bill of health at each police investigation, he would turn on his accuser and demand his money for the trip. On one occasion his accuser spent the evening in a cell because he failed to dig up the price of the ride. It would have broken the cabby's heart to know that he once drove Jim Murray home and that Jim got there safe. This was due to Murray's refusal to drive through the park. Even if the cabby had known Murray, he would probably have thought Jim was an eccentric who played marbles in his old age.

Murray always had a marble or two in his hands and he kept them constantly rolling between his fingers. He would roll them with a contented look on his face and then drop them back into his coat, only to dive into another pocket to pick out another marble and roll that in a peaceful manner. He could never have qualified as the champion boy marble shooter of New Jersey, for the marbles never left his hands. Every marble was a perfect pearl and the biggest was worth $20,000. Murray was a miner who had made his money in Butte, Montana, in the days of Fair, Mackey, Marcus Daly, and the others.

Although Diamond Jim Brady wore a fortune in Oriental pearls at different times, yet Pearl Jim Murray carried from 100 to 200 pearls in his pockets and their value was not less than $1,000,000! He never had them strung or mounted, but loved to roll them in his fingers and seemed to derive great pleasure from their smooth, satiny touch.

It is a remarkable thing about the pearl, that, although it is the manifestation of a sick oyster, yet it is the only precious jewel which is perfect when found. Rubies, diamonds, sapphires, and emeralds must be cut and polished, but the pearl is never touched except to fondle.

I never read of a famous string of pearls without thinking that the man who bored the holes in the jewels had murdered the pearls. They are too marvelous in their original state to be made to suffer from having a hole bored through them. Murray must have thought the same way, for he never wore a pearl in a ring or in his cravat. However, there were others who did not think so. Whenever Mrs. Jackson Gourard appeared in Rector's she wore a string of pearls that was more like a hawser. Lillian Russell and Anna Held were two other ladies who also carried beautiful necklaces of Oriental pearls.

Mrs. George Kessler was another who agreed with Diamond Jim that "Them as has 'em, wears 'em."

If they had them, they wore them in those days, and they were perfectly safe. It was before the time of the thieving finale hopper and the crooked lounge lizard. Jewels were just as safe in Rector's as a corner stone in a town hall. Although some notorious international thieves often dined there, they never operated during their hours of relaxation, even though they may have brought their war maps along to plan future campaigns.

Mistakes Will Happen

The only thing ever stolen in Rector's was a jeweled purse which disappeared on New Year's Eve at the instant we turned out the lights signifying that the old year was gone. When the lights went on, the pocketbook had gone along with the old year. It was returned five years later, when the waiter who had taken it made the second mistake of deserting his wife. She turned informer and wrote to the New York police, who found the purse in a safety-deposit vault in a small town in Massachusetts.

Only one theft in all those years is a remarkable record when you consider the lavish display of jewels, and all the more remarkable when you compare the old days with the new. The wise man or woman never wears his or her jewelry in public these days. If they are fortunate enough to have diamonds, they keep them in a vault and show their prosperity by wearing the keys to the vault around their necks as an indication of their wealth.

Chapter 11

The Great Sport of Eating

Food is an important accessory, especially at meals. No less an athletic authority than Grantland Rice assures us that eating is the greatest of competitive sports. Napoleon said that an army moved on its stomach. As a reward for this culinary epigram, he had a piece of French pastry named after him. Bismarck never said anything about food, but he had a herring named in his honor just the same.

The importance of food in history can readily be recognized when you realize that the Versailles delegates sat down to three dining tables and but one conference table a day. Although Diamond Jim Brady was probably the greatest amateur eater of modern times, he was not the originator of the habit. Many centuries ago the world's great men strove for laurels at the table, as pigs strive at the trough. A full and permanent paunch was considered the visible emblem of health and success. Thin and meagre men were looked upon with suspicion, even the "lean and hungry Cassius." While the fat flourished and grew stouter, the skinny and the hungry waxed frailer and more attenuated.

The feeling of the starved against the satiated was summed up by John Ball in 1360, when he complained, "They have wine and spices and fair bread; and we oatcake and straw, and water to drink." So many must have been of John's opinion that they followed Wat Tyler in his rebellion. Before Wat got his chance to build up on wine and spices, he had the honor of being assassinated by the Lord Mayor of London in the presence of Richard II. It was dangerous to criticize the cooking in those days.

With the exception of Lucullus, the most famous eater of ancient times was probably Charles V of Spain. After a lifetime spent in battling the westward-bound Turk, he retired to his estate at Yuste. Before leaving for the suburbs, he gave Germany to his brother Ferdie and deeded Spain and the Netherlands to his bright son Philip. Having rid himself of all this valuable real estate, he proceeded to devote the rest of his career to eating. One hundred and fifty attendants retired with Charlie to his voluntary Elba, and they all wore chefs' caps and aprons. The ex-emperor wrote daily to the Secretary of State at Valladolid and every letter asked for rare and fancy dishes. Royal couriers speeding from Valladolid to Lisbon were ordered to detour via Jarandilla and bring supplies for the table of Charles who thought that the local trout were too small and demanded bigger ones from better streams.

We are grateful to Charles's appetite, for it gives us the inspiring picture of a king's messenger carrying the fate of a nation under one arm and a fish under the other. Eels, oysters, frogs, and rabbits were conquered and captured all over the known earth and mailed by parcel post to Yuste. He doted on eel potpie and went into conniption fits over anchovies and truffles. He managed to get about six good years of intensive eating before he succumbed. It is remarkable that he lived that long, for a fish does not gain in flavor or odor by taking a long ride on horseback.

Charles existed for his stomach alone during the latter part of his career. History must excuse his imperial piggishness, because he had earned his gastronomical vacation by spending most of his life on the battlefield, chasing and being chased by the valiant Turks. He had earned his meals. The trouble with the folks of to-day is that they acquire their food with too little effort. However, we lazy moderns have the advantage over Charles in that our refrigerating conditions are better. When Rector's sent to the far corners of the earth for a mackerel or a pompano, it arrived as cool and as fresh as a daisy in the rain. We were compelled to scour the globe for delicacies to fan the feather-edged tonsils of our patrons whose appetites were jaded by too much monotony and repetition of menus. The sameness of food, served day after day and month after month, has caused battles in homes, riots in institutions, and rebellions in armies. A continued diet of bread and water is no worse than a prolonged existence on turkey and cranberries. Either one will get you in the end.

It is a terrible feeling to walk sluggishly into your dining room every day, knowing just what is going to be served and seeking some way in which to avoid it. When the tribes of Africa started the neat habit of eating one another it was not so much because of a flair for cannibalism as a desire for a change from the chronic diet of plantains and bananas. There was a theatrical boarding house not far from Rector's where the inmates called mutton 365 because they got it every day in the year. No wonder they went insane during the leap year, when they brooded over that extra day, and bombarded their landlady with a barrage of greasy mutton chops.

A Lamb in Boarding-House Clothing

Did this result in a culinary novelty? It did not. The landlady carefully gathered up the chops, and mutton croquettes were served the next day. Once again the landlady was the target for a shower of mutton in croquette form, and once again she scooped it up. It was on the table the following day in the shape of mutton hash. This proved to be her final attempt to foist mutton on a free and independent people by force of arms or circumstances. No power on earth could put Humpty Dumpty or mutton hash together again. By this time the boarders were barking like sheep dogs and they tore the landlady limb from lamb. The jury decided that it was cold-blooded murder, with extenuating circumstances, and the boarders marched out under their own colors. It may have been a queer verdict. But you can expect anything in a town where a culprit's lawyer once handed in a plea of justifiable bigamy.

I am citing this incident because landladies and chefs are up against the same problem of variation in menus. If Rector's had displayed no more ingenuity than this landlady, we would have been forced to close our doors in a week. We had four separate daily cards—luncheon, tea, dinner, and after-theatre supper. We were not open for breakfast. There was also a fifth card in booklet form. As this was a wine list, we may as well change the subject.

Our efforts to secure a variety in food meant that we had to remain in touch with the universe. No traveler ever took stranger journeys than the Rector market basket. It skidded over the snows in the Russian droshky, climbed the Andes, and bobbed on camels through the Sahara. Travel is educational, but it was saddening to learn that there are no frankfurters in Frankfort. It was with three kinds of astonishment that we heard that there was no chop suey in China. Chop suey is strictly an American idea of Mongolian cuisine.

All we imported from Hong-Kong and Shanghai were swallow's-nest soup, shark fins, pigeon eggs, rice wine, and bamboo shoots. Many of our patrons developed a Chinese slant in food after attending the armistice dinner held to celebrate the end of the warfare between the two powerful tongs of Chinatown, New York. All the tong shootings and murders were within the jurisdiction of Judge Foster. His rulings were so impartial and fair that the tongs asked him to act as go-between during the peace conference. He smoothed out all Celestial bickerings and the tongs signed a Manchurian document that must never have been a peace treaty. I attended the dinner given in honor of Judge Foster by the hatchet and gun men at the Port Arthur restaurant. I don't know what I ate, but to this day I have a suspicion that I dined on a tiger's gizzard, a rhinoceros' ears, and mandarin's beard stuffed with marble dust. From that day to this I have never cared for Old Peking crab waffles or Canton-flannel Eclairs.

When West Meets East

We must give great credit to the Chinese for their earnest, if not Christian, endeavors to secure a varied menu. The small fins of sharks are really delicious if prepared properly. I could supply you with the recipe, but will not, as I think that a bride should stick to her biscuits. Crow's-nest chowder is strictly an Oriental dish and does not live in captivity. I also have the recipe for that, but have been requested by the War Department to keep it a secret. Dragon whiskers in rice-wine sauce is another beautiful dish, but I think that most people would order me to bring on the wine sauce and to bob the whiskers. Hummingbird kidneys with shattered sardines taste very well, and so do green beetles and powdered elephant tusks.

They were all served at Judge Foster's dinner. I attended as a guest and was perfectly satisfied to leave the same way. I expected the hatchet men to revert to their trade at any minute. Vincent Astor also was a guest who did not choose up sides. The dinner was so long ago that I do not recollect the names of the diners, but there were a number of high police officials present. A few minutes after the dinner Judge Foster and I had the pleasure of meeting in a lunch wagon. We dined heartily. I still have a set of inlaid chop sticks which have never been used. No reasonable bid refused.

The patrons of Rector's who dine on shark fins and bamboo shoots were men who were pioneers in Chinese trade and whose calling compelled them to live in the Far East six months of the year. Although there is great variety in the cuisine of the Far East, the Near West is good enough for me. There are many things served in restaurants that the cook is too smart to eat.

We did plunder one Eastern country of its richness, and that land was India. It was from India that we got the famous curries and chutneys. We are indebted to India for curries of chicken, lamb, lobster, sweetbread, and shrimp. Here is the recipe for a famous sauce which garnished curry of chicken à la Rector:

> Chop three medium-sized onions and brown in a quarter of a pound of butter. When brown, add a quarter of a pound of chopped cooked ham, a scant half teaspoonful of celery salt, about two dozen whole black peppercorns, several cloves, and a large pinch of thyme. Cook for about ten minutes and add a quarter of a teaspoonful of salt and two tablespoonfuls of curry powder. Mix thoroughly and add one quart of stock. Cook about twenty minutes. Now take two egg yolks beaten lightly with half a pint of sweet cream and add to curry sauce. Mix well, but do not allow to boil again. Now strain through a fine sieve and add two tablespoonfuls of fresh grated coconut. Then add cooked chicken cut up in pieces about an inch in size and a quarter of an inch thick.

Plain boiled rice and chutney are always served with a curried dish.

Serve the rice separately and allow guests to mix rice in with curry to suit themselves.

Jewels from Russia

The same sauce is used also in all curries of lobster, lamb, sweetbreads, or shrimp. I have taken the presumption of writing it here, although I have no doubt that most housewives already know it. The Bengal chutney is strictly a native Indian dish, as it is a peculiarity of tropical citizens to love hot condiments and peppery foods. The chile con carne of Mexico is plenty of proof of this weakness—or it may be a strength. I suspect that even inhabitants of temperate zones have a fondness for hot dishes. In fact, I became convinced of this after once having served an irritable New Englander with a tureen of cold clam chowder. He arrived in the kitchen only a belligerent jump behind the waiter.

We raided Russia for its most important dainty, beluga caviar, which is taken from its original owner, the large sturgeon. The sturgeon is trapped alive and then confined in a small tank. As the fish is always caught when it is on its way upstream to spawn, it is held in pawn until the eggs grow larger. Then the sturgeon roe is removed by an expert and the eggs are salted. The caviar is very perishable and must be kept packed in ice.

Berlin was the caviar market in the old days and may still hold its scepter. It shipped its caviar all over the world. The pure-food laws allow packers to use only benzoate of soda as a preservative of foods, and then only to the extent of a hundredth of one per cent. We were up against a problem in the old days, as benzoate of soda was apt to sour the delicate caviar on its way to market. We fought for years to induce Doctor Wiley to permit us to substitute boracic acid for benzoate of soda, but the good doctor always withheld his official permission.

I have always thought the doctor was wrong in this one case, as in my judgment boracic acid is much less harmful than the benzoate. Beluga caviar is the brightest of the crown jewels of Russia and seems to be the only one that has not been taken out of circulation by the Bolshevists.

Another famous Russian institution is borsch, which is not a cathedral, castle, or native dance, but a soup. Borsch is to Russia what clam chowder is to New England. Everybody eats it, and those who don't eat it rub it into their hair. It fed hundreds of millions of Russians during the last few years of famine. There are different grades of borsch. The poorest kind made by the peasants is brewed from red beets and water with beef stock added. Aristocratic borsch, as served in Rector's for many years, is distilled thus:

> Prepare for roasting two Long Island ducks. Place in very hot oven and allow to brown, not to cook. Remove the ducks from the oven and put them in a large pot containing water. The water should be cold. Boil slowly for five or six hours. Take the ducks out of the pot. What remains in the pot is the consommé of the fowl. Into this consommé grate a dozen fair-sized cooked beets. Strain the consommé through a very fine sieve. Clarify the consommé by the use of the white of an egg. It should be a deep-purple color. It is served piping hot to each guest, along with a small pitcher of sour cream. As the soup is served the guest drops the sour cream in the dish.

This is the national soup of Russia.

At first we used to import Spanish and Portuguese sardines, but later on we changed to those that come from the northern waters of France. Sardines grow harder and firmer in the cooler waters of the Atlantic. As a matter of fact, France supplied us with most of our rare and intricate table delicacies. I have already mentioned truffles, mushrooms, *pâté de foie gras,* and Burgundy snails.

There was another novelty which attracted much attention some years ago. This was a monstrous apple. The French farmer would strip his tree of all apples except a dozen. All the force and growth of the tree went into these dozen apples instead of being diffused among a thousand. Photographic negatives of Washington, Lincoln, and Roosevelt were placed on the apples while they were still green. The sun would do the developing of the negatives during the summer and the result would be apples bearing pictures of these famous Americans. We served them on national holidays, much to our patrons' astonishment.

All our cheeses were imported from France with the exception of Limburger, and New York cheeses from Herkimer County. We tried one experiment with Persian cheese made from goat's milk. It was fortunate for us that we opened the cheese in the cellar. The rich goaty perfume automatically rang seventeen fire-alarm gongs and our kitchen crew stampeded upstairs to the street. In all my career, spent in inhaling the odors of frying and stewing, I had never had that experience. Persian goat cheese is the ancestor of all odors. We immediately withdrew our ambassador from Persia and severed diplomatic food relations. We had a foreign representative who did nothing but travel through Europe in search of queer things to eat. He was advised by cable to stay out of Asia.

To be Served on Blotters

We went far afield when we imported the African peach from Algiers. This peach arrived around January, at a time when the Delaware and Georgia fruit was well out of season. It was a magnificent peach, golden and luscious. We served it in a cone-shaped glass about a foot high. The peach was peeled and then dropped into the glass. It was then drowned in a pint of champagne. The diner would then drink the champagne and the glass would be refilled. Each peach would stand three pints of champagne before it was eaten. The glass was about six inches wide at the top, and I assure you that it was a very pleasant channel to swim. It was also very costly, as each peach would average around ten dollars when complete with champagne and other accessories. Champagne seemed to be the fitting bath for all food in those days. We had one guest who always insisted on having his ham cooked in champagne sauce. He had a friend who claimed that champagne sauce did not flavor the ham in the least. He said that he could cook a ham in ink and that it would taste just as well as one stewed in champagne. After much argument the experiment was finally tried out in a famous buffet in Washington. I might state that one of the contestants was formerly postmaster-general of the United States. The other was an ex-congressman.

The champagne was easy to procure at that time but all the stationery and drug stores of the District of Columbia were stripped of their bottles of ink.

Finally enough ink was procured to fill a tin bucket. Another pail was filled with champagne and a whole ham was dropped in each. They were placed on a hot stove and simmered side by side for hours. The aroma of hot, evaporating ink permeated the city for miles around. The champagne threw off a dignified, spicy bouquet which caused lawmakers on Capitol Hill to sniff the air in pre-war suspicion, and mules in the far Virginia hills slanted their ears to the north and pulled their wagons with new vigor. At the end of the day it was found that the ink dried so rapidly that it cost more than the champagne. When the experiment was concluded the contest was called a draw. The inky ham tasted just as well as its more stylish brother.

Economical Extravagance

We will explain the joker in the deck. The man who bet on the inky ham knew that the fat of a pig protects the meat from all outside poisons. We know that the bite of a rattlesnake has no more effect on a Kentucky razorback than the bite of a hoss fly has on a locomotive. The hog lets the snake get tired of biting and then proceeds to stamp it into the ground at leisure. I tasted both the ink and the champagne ham, and there was no difference. I might state that the frequent rounds of glasses which passed while the experiment was going on were not filled with ink. They did contain a writing fluid that makes you write home and state that you will not be home that night.

There was a ham from Spain which was in demand. This is the ham of the wild boar of the Iberian Peninsula. It was carved in thin, transparent slices and was served on breast of guinea hen. But there was a greater demand for Virginia ham served with risotto of rice. I might warn you that if you care to experiment on ham cooked in ink, make certain that you use a whole ham protected by its inch of fat. Sliced ham would speedily absorb all the ink and you might as well try to chew a busy bookkeeper's pen wiper.

Another far land which supplied Rector's with unusual dishes was Egypt. The Egyptian quail and partridge had considerable vogue for a while. But they could not be compared with American quail in anything except price. We had to bring them over from the Nile in cold storage, with the result that they lost their flavor, if they ever had any. Some of our patrons insisted on Egyptian quail in a loud, expensive voice, but they were the type of men who love to display their wealth and power by dragging their moustaches through the most costly of soup.

In fact, like Sherry's and Delmonico's, the Rector menu was based more on the vanity than the palate of our diners. There was one lady who ordered strawberries in January. These strawberries came from southern Europe and cost fifty cents each. She would nibble one berry and then order the rest sent back to the icebox. As she held the fruit aloft on a fork she looked all around the room to make sure that everybody saw her. She ate there every night, and one box of berries would last her for a month. It was a rare case of combining economy with extravagance. She didn't care any more for hothouse berries than a leopard cares to chew a wet whisk broom. She ordered them just to make her neighbors jealous.

Whenever we heard a man ordering Egyptian quail in a broadcasting voice we could generally tell that he was a salesman trying to make an impression on his out-of-town buyers. Although we served English pheasant, it could not be compared with the grouse from the Adirondacks. Nevertheless, the English bird outsold its American cousin two to one. There was a snobbishness in those days which demanded a foreign label on its packages. I think that we have outgrown that now, as we realize that home industries and products are not only better but cheaper. With Florida and California growing practically every known fruit, the only things we are forced to import from the Old World are red noses and Egyptian mummies.

Even alligator pears, guava jelly, and other tropical foods are now raised in Florida while we formerly were forced to buy them in the West Indies and South America. Bamboo also is raised in that state. It wasn't so long ago that all bamboo shoots were exclusively Chinese property. I don't know just exactly whether the Floridian shoot is eating bamboo or not, although I guess that bamboo is bamboo when it isn't a chair leg or something else.

California invaded foreign rights when it started to produce the artichoke and the endive. Twenty years ago France had the full monopoly on both these salads. We were absolutely dependent on the incoming French liners for most of our fancy vegetables and greens. The best melon we could get in those days was the Canadian, eight or ten inches in diameter. This has been supplanted by the delicious native honeydew melon and the Casaba. And so far as meats were concerned, American beef always did lead the world. As there are exceptions to rules, I must admit that Southdown mutton from the Sussex district of England was of the finest.

It would have been possible for us to roll along very nicely without a single importation of European delicacies, but, as I have stated, we utilized foreign dishes as bait for the vanity of the snobs—and they bit fast and often. Of course there were many people who had grown accustomed to these things abroad, but they were generally the men who gave the big dinner parties. They demanded everything just so. With the others we did not have to be careful. Everything could be so-so.

I remember one dinner given by Andrew Freedman, builder of subways and then owner of the New York Giants. This dinner was given to celebrate the opening of the first subway on Manhattan Island. The guests were men who were closely connected with the financing of the project and also the engineers who designed the sub. One hundred celebrants sat at a long table laid out to represent the entire subway line. Little toy trains ran along the tracks, carrying the guests' food and drink. There was a guest at each station and his signal lamp was a bottle of champagne. The trains were perfect mechanical models and a live third rail ran down the center of the banquet board. A little dinner like this cost only around ten thousand dollars.

A Good System Gone Wrong

The heaviest dinner check ever picked up was gathered in by Reggie Vanderbilt, who celebrated his coming of age with a stag party. Among the guests were Monte and Larry Waterbury, famous poloists, Foxhall Keene, Eddie and Billie von der Koch, Malcolm and Louis Livingston. All the diners were drawn together by their common love of ponies and four-in-hand driving. They were the finest amateur whips in the world.

There have been many rumors about the closing of Canfield's, but the money lost there by a young millionaire was the real cause. His parents got busy when they heard of it and brought tremendous pressure down on Mr. Canfield.

The raid on Canfield's was under the personal direction of William Travers Jerome, famous district attorney who conducted the Thaw case. He decided to make it a day's work while he was about it, and made a tour of Honest John Kelly's, Davy Johnson's, Daly's, Westcott's and about twenty others. From that night to this day there has not been a roulette wheel in New York City. Jerome went on record by saying that no roulette wheel was on the level, and he was almost right. Jerome was going so strong in those days that they called him the pocket edition of Roosevelt. He drove them all out, big and little.

I have played roulette at Monte Carlo, Biarritz, and Trouville. I had a splendid system if it hadn't been for the fact that I always lost. The system was given to me by one of my college professors, who worked it out on a wheel, but it must have been a cart wheel. He perfected it in the seclusion of his study and assured me that it was unbeatable. The Monte Carlo croupiers may have been uneducated, but their reach was longer than mine. The wheels may have been crooked, but we all know the story about the old-timer who spent his time and money in playing roulette in a Denver gambling palace. One of his friends told him that the wheel was crooked. He retorted sadly, "I know it. But it's the only wheel in town."

The Horsey Dinner

Getting back to the dinners, I think the smartest one was given by C. K. G. Billings, owner of the illustrious trotter, Lou Dillon. The dinner was held at Sherry's and the guests were all on horseback. The ladies rode sidesaddle and the gentlemen cross-saddle. The tables were seven feet high and, of course, there were no chairs. The waiters were on foot. The problem of getting the horses in was almost as difficult as getting the guests out. Although the stunt got immense publicity, I suspect that it was a very uncomfortable dinner, as the steeds developed a natural appetite for celery, ignored the soup and meat, but insisted on sharing the salads with the ladies and gentlemen. The nags must have been terribly disappointed when dessert consisted of orange sherbet instead of baled hay. However, they got some good bites in on the lump sugar. Any time I invite a mounted cop to dinner at my house, I insist on him parking his horse outside in the vestibule.

Then there was the fishermen's dinner given by Jerome Siegel. Among the guests equipped with rod and reel were Lillian Russell, Valeska Surratt, Nora Bayes, Lord Fitzgerald and his cronies, Tommy Lipton and Lord Dewar, Nat Goodwin, Wilton Lackaye, most of the Shuberts, and about every famous theatrical name that used incandescent lights for ink. The table was a hollow square, with the tank in the center. Live trout sparkled and speckled in the tank and everybody was forced to catch his or her own dinner.

It was a question whether the theatrical or the horse clique was the gayer in Broadway night life. The polo bunch always put on an extra sprint during Horse Show Week, and I guess they earned the honors of the year. There was never any seven days like Horse Show Week in New York. Remember that I am speaking of the days when it was no disgrace to be run over by a horse and wagon and when there was always plenty of parking space for bicycles. A dollar went farther in those days even if the headache did not last as long. The week was one long whirl of dinners and entertainments.

Madison Square Garden was decorated at enormous expense and society flocked there from all over the country.

Some of the exhibitors were Judge Moore, Frank Gould, Harry Payne Whitney, George Watson, and our old friend Foxhall Keene, who rode his own jumpers.

It taxed our ingenuity to supply novelties in food during Horse Show Week, and I guess Sherry's and Delmonico's were in the same fix. But I imagine we managed to strike a fairly good average for good food and wines. We figured that the honor of the establishment was at stake with every meal served. There was only one dinner in which we fell into a slump. That was the dinner given by members of the Lambs Club to Harry Woodruff, the star of Brown of Harvard. The guests numbered forty-four. Woodruff was a fine-looking man and was at one time rumored to be engaged to Anna Gould.

I remember the food served at Woodruff's dinner because we received special written instructions from the Lambs present. At that time Rector's was known as the Lambs Annex. The Lambs who had been suspended from their club for a week or a month always joined Rector's.

There were some days when our membership was larger than the parent club.

We got so that we used to suspend the members ourselves. A famous comedian was a member of Rector's for one year and running. He had been suspended from the Lambs for that period for sweeping the glassware off the bar with a very fine Malacca cane. He crashed a magnificent array of cut glass to the floor with one dignified sweep. After his suspension was up he went back to the club and met a friend at the bar. His friend asked him where he had been.

The actor replied, "I was suspended for a year."

The friend asked, "What for?"

"This." And with the remark, the comedian swung the same fine Malacca cane over the bar and again splintered a beautiful collection of glasses on the floor. He renewed his membership in Rector's for another season.

Lone-Wolf Eccentricities

It is usual to start a well-ordered dinner by first serving *canapés* of caviar and anchovies. This being the case, we omitted them altogether at the Woodruff dinner and served nothing. The next course was soup, which was served cold. The oysters were warm. So was the celery, and the olives were red-hot. The fish was frozen stiff and impossible to bite, much less eat. The meat was served all right, but when a guest tried to salt or pepper it, the tops came off the shakers and the meat was deluged with cayenne pepper and salt. The salad consisted of old banana skins and rubber bands. The coffee was served in tin cups and the cigars were the finest stumps we could find in an exclusive neighborhood. The ice cream was stuffed with absorbent cotton. If any guest asked for a serviette the waiter would bring in a piece of burlap bag.

This remarkable dinner was almost equaled by an eccentric character who actually ate all his dinners backward, starting with coffee and reversing through the entire menu, finally winding up with oysters. He always dined alone and never varied his culinary routine. I used to get seasick watching him eat.

Another lone diner was a South American who ordered a double carafe of beer and four portions of ice cream. To my amazement, he dropped the ice cream into the beer and then drank the mixture. A queer diet for a lone wolf.

We had many solitary guests who strode in night after night, sat at a table and brooded amidst the laughter and conversation. It would be an accurate guess to judge them to be men with domestic or financial troubles or lawyers figuring out intricate problems.

There was one lonely patron who stuck out like a pump handle on a farm. You could spot him farther than a shipwrecked sailor can see a lighthouse. He wore three kinds of full dress. One was a vivid blue, one was red, and the third was grayish green.

He came into Rector's for years and had what we might call the right of way. That is, none of the boisterous regulars ever insulted him or called attention to his garb. Nobody ever knew who he was, although a cabby informed us that the mysterious blue-red-and-green stranger lived at the Plaza Hotel, which was as costly as it was exclusive. No man or woman ever dined with the tricolored hermit. A full-dress suit is terrible enough without being forced to see one in bright red.

I have already mentioned Dan Daly, who dined alone on snails and champagne. But he had a reason, for he was a very sick man. Every organization or club has its member who doesn't fraternize and insists on spending his nights sunk to his hubs in the deepest and best Morris chair.

Such a man always casts a chill over me. It is best illustrated in a theatre. Drop one single grouch in a row of happy people and he will envelop them all in gloom. Try it yourself some time. You will be able to freeze an entire row in the audience.

I may be wrong about this. But it was my business to see that everybody in our establishment was happy. Therefore a frowning face was a challenge to me. Possibly all the other diners were too busy to notice one exception. There was another single guest who always came in alone and always left alone. He was the jolly man about town who knew everybody in the place, and before the evening was over he would have made the rounds of the tables, nibbled at many a chafing dish, and sampled numerous free drinks. He enjoyed himself immensely, was a good story-teller, and never allowed the fun to simmer down. But when the check arrived he was on his way to another group of friends at another table. He would flirt gently with the ladies at a table, but never openly enough to risk a quarrel. The queer thing about this type is that he was always welcome in spite of the fact that he was looking out of the window when the waiter arrived with the total of bad news. The waiters were wise to him and never bothered him with the bill. However, he added to the gayety of nations like a paper hat at a birthday party.

It takes one of every kind to make a world, but it's worse when they're twins. The man who runs an omnibus must expect to carry all kinds of passengers just so long as somebody pays the fare. Green full dress, men about tables, and individuals who ate their dinner backward must fit into the scheme of things somewhere. We could tell just what eccentricities our patrons would develop after being seated at the table, and didn't care much, provided they paid the check and left without a declaration of war.

A Water-Marked Check

Sometimes, after a man had dined heartily, we were confronted with the problem of collecting the price of the meal. Very often he might have left his pocketbook at home on the usual convenient piano. If we knew him we would take his personal check. If he couldn't identify himself and seemed sincere, there was nothing to do but show him the door in a courteous manner. If we thought he was trying to defraud us we might threaten him with arrest. But we never accepted a stranger's check after a sad experience with one drawn on the Bank of Lake Erie. That bank must have been in the lake. All restaurants must charge this loss up to experience. Some people make a practice of defrauding restaurants in this manner, but have never met with much success in an automat.

We had at least five hundred charge accounts for years, with practically no loss. Each one of the five hundred was entitled to sign his dinner tabs, which meant we always had a considerable sum out on speculation. This system may seem as loose as a shirt on a shad, but the only time we lost an account was when a tab signer had met with financial reverses in business. The restaurant proprietor of to-day has a decided edge on the old-timers. Now it is possible to attach a patron's motor car and secure the money. In those times all we could attach was a bicycle.

You must take risks in all businesses and bad checks are included in the hazards. However, the paper hanger who follows this precarious means of livelihood generally has a career shorter than Tom Thumb's bed. He is soon getting his consommé strained through iron bars, which operation doesn't improve the soup or his chances of escape.

Chapter 12

Home Cooking

No matter how rich and successful we become in life the best we can hope for is what the vagrant calls three squares and a flop, meaning three good meals a day and a place to sleep. No man has more and no man should have less. The vernacular of the panhandler is the sum total of existence.

Rector's did its best to see that man got his three squares a day. In this respect the home is also a restaurant, with the exception that it has a smaller clientele. We might paraphrase an old proverb and say that when bad cooking comes in the window love flies up the dumbwaiter shaft. One advantage that dining out has over home cooking is you can take your choice in a restaurant, while at home you must either like it or lump it.

It is amazing how many thousands of restaurants advertise so-called home cooking. After eating this home cooking you know the answer to why girls leave home. Home cooking must have been a greatly overrated institution for years. You realize this when you note how many modern homes seem to be able to get along without it. The old-fashioned kitchen has been replaced by the kitchenette, which in turn is about to be supplanted by the serving pantry—a shrunken alcove about as large as a telephone booth, but not so comfortable. I defy any woman to get a biscuit out of a serving pantry without breaking an arm. Like many other unfortunates who are doomed to spend their lives in great cities I have just leased an apartment with a serving pantry just large enough to act as a kennel for one solitary frankfurter. There is an icebox about as big as a medicine chest and an electric stove small enough to be of platinum.

Fortunately we are within crawling distance of a delicatessen store and we have become expert enough to cook our eggs by holding matches to them. Our bread arrives from an enormous bakery filled with machinery. It is not like Mother used to make. It is better. Mother was no mechanic.

It is not necessary for a bride to know about cooking to-day. Every known variety of food is now put up in tins, and a woman can do all her cooking with a can opener. However, there is one pleasant feature about home cooking—we get it without a cover charge.

Origin of the Cover Charge

The present cover charge is a war tax laid on hopeful diners to defray the loss by evaporation of certain contraband liquids. The night clubs also impose this nocturnal assessment to assist them in paying the salaries of whispering barytones, laughing trombonists, and soprano hostesses. It was introduced into America by J. B. Martin, of the Jean Baptiste Martin café. Practically all the restaurants of Paris have always fined their patrons an extra franc to cover the depreciation in china and glassware and also for the bread and butter service. This was known as the *couvert* charge and amounted to about twenty cents a person.

When the Café Martin inaugurated the habit in America we nabbed the idea, but raised the ante to twenty-five cents a cover. The sole reason for the charge was for B and B, known in the rural districts as bread and butter. When

Florenz Ziegfeld opened his illustrious Midnight Frolic on the Amsterdam Roof, his audience sat at tables and chairs instead of the orthodox orchestra seats. Ziggy served a very good meal with his roof operettas; there was a space for dancing and also a wine list.

I am again singing the song of the dear old days beyond recall; also beyond referendum. However, history is history, wet or dry. The tables were bought at the box office just like theatre tickets, because Ziggy had a theatrical and a concert license. But when the modern cabarets opened with their rival singing-and-dancing attractions they were unable to sell tickets for their tables because it would be a violation of city ordinances and fire laws pertaining to places of amusement and restaurants.

No cabaret can sell tickets for its tables. That is where the *couvert* charge stepped in. It was raised to five and ten dollars to cover the thousands of dollars spent by the owners in entertainment and decoration. There is one night club in New York which has a cover charge of twenty-five hard dollars. This is merely the admission charge. You can get real champagne for another twenty-five a bottle. That is, it is as real as cider and carbonated water can make it. There is also pre-war gin about a week old. The patrons pay heavily for this. The customers sit around their tables all night, listening to the ribald singing, drinking bad wine, and inhaling an atmosphere consisting mostly of rice powder and spots before the eyes. This is what is known in the big cities as life. If this is life I will take Patrick Henry's second choice. Curiously enough the price of the liquor is jotted down on the check as B and B.

There is one well-known rounder who consumes $100 worth of bread and butter every night. A millionaire loves to frequent night clubs, which are known to the wise crackers as deadfalls, drums, and flea bags. He was handed a check totaling $800 for a few rounds of drinks for four people. He shoved the check back, saying, "I may be crazy, but not that crazy."

He didn't pay the check. But he must have been crazy again the next evening for he paid one twice as heavy. When a patron refuses to meet the exorbitant rates charged by some night clubs the usual procedure is for a couple of muscular waiters to frisk him. If he has no money on him they boot him around until he stops bouncing. No proprietor of a flea bag is foolish enough to accept a personal check, because he knows it will be stopped at the bank in the morning. He knows his game is outlawed and he has no redress for nonpayment. Therefore if he cannot get cash he dismisses his patron with a warning and a black eye to remember it. The food served in these drums is mostly chop suey or any Chinese dish that can be mixed in a hat. Nobody goes there to eat in the first place.

Most of these hide-aways are located in reconstructed cellars which are too damp and gloomy for the usual plumbing shops or local express offices. They are best described by an expert Broadwayite as upholstered sewers. They are decorated to the queen's bad taste. I have been in many of them, but not to drink. I like pump water, but I do not like to put my head under the pump the next morning.

These places cannot be described as restaurants, as they do business under night-club charters. They have kitchens, but the chef's patron saint is Lucrezia Borgia. The bright scholars will remember Lucrezia. She was the only woman who never lost her temper when the cook broke expensive Venetian glassware. In fact, Lucrezia used to break a few glasses herself and dropped the pulverized fragments into the food. None of her guests were ever on the committee which reported progress.

The only guest who ever escaped from one of her meals was a Genoese admiral who accepted her dinner invitation, but had judgment enough to bring his marines with him. Meals in those days were more dangerous than battles. A general invited to a Roman banquet usually drew his sword, placed it conveniently on the table and said, "Pardon me, Nero, if I eat with my knife." High officials never knew whether the tablecloth would be hanging on the washline the next morning or flying at half-mast on the town hall. They all arrived in sedan chairs carried by four slaves, indicating that they had enough sense to bring their pallbearers along.

Sometimes the old-timers forgot their quarrels and gathered together for a real imperial spread. Then they hung up new Olympic records for gluttony. These dinners were progressive affairs, going from bad to worse. When the tribunes and the consuls had glutted themselves they motioned feebly for attendants armed with peacock feathers. If you have ever had your tonsils tickled with a peacock feather you can imagine the result. In a few minutes the guests were ready to start eating all over again.

We had many famous feasts in Rector's, but none to compare with the Banquet on the Bridge sponsored by that eminent host Caligula. The festival celebrated the opening of the bridge spanning the water from Puteoli to Misenum. Lunch was served in the middle of the bridge, and then the guests found themselves in the middle of the bay. Caligula had them all kicked overboard to drown. They might have liked the cooking, but they could not have cared much for the sauce.

The Roman remembered best for his feasts was Lucullus, whose homes in Naples and Misenum were the scenes of great feasts. His full title was Lucius Licinius Lucullus, which makes him the original Luke McLuke. Anyway Luke was so fond of sea food that he had salt-water fish brought all the way to his fish ponds in the hills and stationed a slave there to see that the fish got the proper attention. The slave carried a saltcellar and gave the fish a pinch of salt every hour on the hour. Like all saltcellars the darned thing wouldn't work on rainy days, and Luke decided to dig a canal through the mountains to the sea. He did this, and salt water flowed from the Mediterranean to Luke's family pond.

Luke's Guest of Honor

Luke put on more lugs than any other Roman patrician. Pompey and his boy friend Cicero dropped in on Luke Lukius one day, trying to catch him off his epicurean guard. They thought they had him euchred when they suggested that all they wanted was the simple repast he had prepared for himself. Luke agreed to this, only asking that he be allowed to tell his servant the room in which to serve the free lunch. He got their permission and told his man to dish up the food in the Apollo Room. The dinner cost Luke exactly $10,000 because no meal was ever set in the Apollo Room for less than that amount. But it was worth it, for he had fooled Pompey and Cicero.

Luke hated to dine alone, but when he did, he did it in style. A new butler from a Carthaginian employment agency was ordered to serve a solitary meal for Luke, and made the mistake of using paper and picnic plates under the impression that Luke didn't mind, provided the neighbors didn't see it. Luke kicked the butler out of his toga and said, "Sappio, dost thee not knoweth that to-day Lucullus dineth with Lucullus?"

He ordered his purple biscuits to be spread in the fabled Herculanean Hall of Mirrors, where he could look up from his soup and see a thousand other Lukes looking up from their soup. He had one slave whose sole duty was to stand at Luke's right hand at every banquet and tell Luke when he was approaching the limit of indulgence in rich foods. When this slave figured that Luke was overeating he would grab his master's wrist and Luke's evening was over.

All of us have this same kind of overseeing if we would exercise it. In our case the slave's name is Moderation, and we should let him have his sway at all times lest our appetites become a bevy of Circes to transform us into human swine. Luke might have been an epicurean, but he was no gourmand whose eyes were bigger than his stomach. He was typical of the decadent days of the Roman Republic, except that he exercised restraint. Rome decayed when wine and viands took the place of water and oatmeal. The nation that had conquered all nations with its sword finally conquered itself with its teeth.

A Great Little Guy

There is intemperance in food as well as in drink. America is a temperate nation in its eating. I was in the restaurant game for twenty-two years and I know my book. We can look at our successful men of to-day for proof of this. Twenty years ago the rich man was of the fat type. John W. Gates, Diamond Jim Brady, Dan Reid, and the elder Morgan were very paunchy. The corporation monarch of to-day is on a diet. John D. Rockefeller, Henry Ford, and Elbert H. Gary are thin enough to be poor. They will outlive their stout predecessors two years to one. The business man of to-day is a light eater.

One of the lightest eaters I know of is George M. Cohan. He could fly like an eagle on the diet of a sparrow. He hasn't gained a pound of weight in twenty years. If he had been a cadet in West Point in 1900 he could still wear the same uniform to-day without alteration. I consider him the most important man on the American stage to-day. I owe him a lifelong gratitude for one thing he did for us around 1911. My father and I had just finished building the new Hotel Rector. As I said before, the French farce, *The Girl from Rector's,* had effectually killed the hotel and it was withering on the vine. Another bad feature was that in building the hotel and new restaurant we had lost the old homey atmosphere of the old Rector's, and Broadway resented it. We were closed a year during the building of the modern establishment, and Churchill's, Shanley's, Murray's, and the Café de l'Opera sprung up in the interim and took away our entire clientele. For three months there wasn't one guest in the 250-room hotel, our restaurant trade was nil, and our bar registered zero. We were losing $1,000 a day. George came into the grill one evening after a tour, looked around at the empty tables and said, "Good-evening, George. Where is the crowd?"

"Good-evening, George," I replied. "There is not, has not and may not be a crowd."

Now there could not be anything more dull than a conversation between two men named George unless one of the men happened to be George M. Cohan. I told him about the effect of Paul Potter's play on the Hotel Rector. He put his arm around my shoulder and invited me to have dinner with him.

After dinner we smoked cigars and he said: "George, I don't like to see this. Rector's has always been a great little place, you're a great little guy, and I always liked you both. I'm going to show you that I'm a great little guy. I'm going to live in your hotel and so are my friends. I'm going to eat in your restaurant again and so are all my pals. Get me a suite of rooms on the Second floor, facing on Broadway. I'm going to live here by the year. You're a great little guy."

And he went out saying, "You're a great little guy," meanwhile shaking his head in the affirmative. He stopped at the door to say, "Your hotel is going to be filled to-morrow. You're a great little guy. So am I."

He kept his word and took a five-room suite in Rector's, even though he already had an apartment in the Hotel Knickerbocker leased by the year. Our hotel was completely filled inside of a week. George moved in bag, baggage, and piano. He would bang that piano at all hours of the night and on it he composed Mary Is a Grand Old Name, Yankee Doodle Dandy, Give My Regards to Broadway, and a hundred other tunes which swept the country. He was a warm friend and his greatest tribute to anybody was, "You're a great little guy."

He was the center of the New York he sang about so delightfully. He was joking when he said, "I'm a great little guy, too," but I never heard a truer word. George never forgot a friend who helped in the days around 1900, when the Four Cohans were struggling to get a chance to show their ability on Broadway. George could do anything that anyone else could do on the stage—and do it better. Although he came from good theatrical stock he admits himself that he started with nothing but complete confidence in his own ability. He sang without a voice and danced without steps. The result was he created the George M. Cohan school of acting, and has more imitators than any man in the world. His success was earned. He might have been twenty years on Broadway, but he was twenty years getting there. His songs are sung the world over, the greatest being Over There, which became the battle song of the A. E. F. Joseph Tumulty, who was President Woodrow Wilson's secretary, wrote to George and told him that President Wilson considered Over There the war's greatest inspiration to American manhood.

Lackaye's Definition of Tact

George trouped with his father, mother, and sister for many years and has a fund of anecdotes of the days on the road. He sat in Rector's night after night, hashing up old times in the tanks and jerk-waters. I think the funniest story he tells is of life in theatrical boarding houses. George lived for one night in a boarding house run by Mother O'Brien. He says that the establishment was run on two rules, these rules being not to smoke hop in the parlor and to bury your own dead. It was an old Colonial building with but one bathroom for all, which was a reminder of Wilton Lackaye's definition of tact. His idea of real tact is a gentleman, opening the door of a bathroom, seeing a lady in the tub, backing out of the room, closing the door, meanwhile saying, "Excuse me, Sir."

About that time George was engaged in his first attempt at song writing, the result being a melodious epitaph entitled Why Did Nellie Leave Her Home? The question was never answered, even though George sang it off key to every publisher in New York. It was written to waltz time, punctuated by explosions of dynamite in the new subway excavation running up Broadway. The work of composing the song required great quiet—which was not furnished by the troupe of acrobats and wire walkers in the next room who were playing stud poker and apparently using stove lids for chips. The stud game was not much of a success, many of the losers suffering from the fact that the subway blasts shook the building and turned over their hole cards.

George's musical career was further hampered by the fact that Singer had twenty of his midgets rooming in Mother O'Brien's, and they were all parked in one bed in the room overhead. When one midget turned over they all had to turn over, with the result that the end midget generally fell out of bed. Princess Rajah and her snakes were also neighbors. The snakes had the clubby habit of getting loose from their baskets and crawling all over the hostelry.

Ringing a Dumb-Bell

The best room was occupied by Ferry the Frog Man, a front bender of great ability. He was a sleepless man who lay awake nights thinking up new and queer methods of contorting his spine. When he got a new idea he would rise, don his frog outfit with a monstrous head and incandescent eyes and try out his new creations on the chandelier. He had lifted himself to the chandelier and hung there for a few minutes revolving and twisting until he managed to get himself into a splendid knot, with his legs twice around his neck, his arms twice around his legs and his spine in a combination diamond hitch and a running bowline. But he didn't realize that he had accidentally turned on a gas jet while hanging on the chandelier, with the result that he was rapidly becoming drowsy.

Ajax the Strong Man had the room next to Ferry and had just rung for ice water by dropping a hundred-pound dumb-bell on the floor. Mother O'Brien was shuffling with the pitcher of ice water, but missed Ajax's room in her hurry, opening Ferry's door. She looked up and saw a monstrous reptile coiled around the chandelier and published the finest scream ever heard in the theatrical district. This aroused Ferry, but frightened him so that he forgot the solution to his tangling puzzle and started to wave his arms and legs in an effort to unwind himself. Then the gas got in its work and Ferry went to sleep again round the chandelier.

Mother O'Brien dashed into Rajah's room and made a hurried exit with six real boa constrictors wriggling after her. One of the boas made a bee, or rather snake, line for the midgets' room with the apparent idea of laying in a food supply for the winter. Another snake got into the bathroom and slept in the tub. Ching Ling Foo, the magician, came in to take a plunge and turned on the hot water. This aroused the snake, and when Ching saw its head above the tub he cancelled his American tour by way of a window, a fire escape, and a second-class passage.

The firemen and police arrived about the same time and started to bring chaos out of disorder by arguing with one another. George was meanwhile engrossed in his composition and making hay while the moon shone by adding all the new and strange noises to his orchestration. The law was making good progress until the half-boiled snake crawled out of the tub looking for the fool who had turned on the water. One fireman went down the stairs on Joe Jackson's bicycle and the midgets ran around like little pink-and-white puddings, getting underfoot and in great danger of being flattened out by the ponderous police. As one copper said later, "We was knee-deep in midgets."

Mother O'Brien had fainted while Princess Rajah was collecting her boas and came to just as the firemen were dragging a hose through the hall. Mother saw the hose running past her door and even to this day is convinced that she saw a hundred-foot boa with a white skin and gleaming brass joints. There was no fire, so the firemen bent their efforts to unbending Ferry. He was in a terrific knot, and it was first feared they would have to cut him into pieces and sew him together again right. However, after fifty minutes of effort, they got him untied and put him to bed.

But Ferry had ruined Cohan's evening, because the gas was supplied by a quarter slot machine. The lights went out just when George was on his second chorus and he finished it in the dark, playing half the tune on the piano and the other half on the bureau. He claims the reason why no musician ever plays Why Did Nellie Leave Her Home? correctly is that they limit their efforts to the piano alone. In order to get the real spirit into the music it is necessary to play half of it on the piano and the other half on a bureau.

Chapter 13

Old-Time Snicks and Snacks

Allowing for some slight exaggeration the foregoing is almost an average account of life in the old-time theatrical boarding houses. Magicians, opera singers, bell ringers, acrobats, trained seals, and equally trained fleas all lived together in harmonious discord and fraternal uproar. When the actors were laying off and funds were low Mother O'Brien would carry the boys along until times got better. She even winked at her own rules and allowed the tenants to cook over gas-jets.

An actor with the bare price of a cheap breakfast would split it two ways with a less fortunate brother. And when neither had funds, they could always sneak into Considine's Metropole and shag some free lunch. Considine's had three entrances and a man thrown out of one door could always come in another. George Considine was a very husky citizen and usually acted as master of ceremonies in his own barroom. He ejected one intoxicated gentleman who was too boisterous and told him not to come back again. Considine took him on a personally conducted tour to the door and dropped him for a field goal on the sidewalk. Then he walked back, rubbing his hands in the reflective manner of a man who has just done something well worth doing. To his surprise he saw the drunk coming in another door opening on the side street.

Considine grabbed him by the scruff and tossed him out, saying, "Didn't I tell you not to come back?" Five minutes later the same well-lubricated lad staggered through a third door, and as Considine started for him he backed out, exclaiming, "Good heavens, do you own all the places in town?"

Considine and the other café owners experienced great difficulties with the itinerant actors and Broadwayites who came in to sample the free lunch without first going through the formality of sampling the beer. The barkeeps kept an eagle eye on the food show and woe to the man who tried to eat himself fat after buying one or no beers. It was another of those famous unwritten laws that no client could attack the lunch counter until he had purchased two beers at five cents apiece. Having complied with this invisible mandate a man could stroll casually over to the free lunch, pick out a reasonably clean fork, and start stabbing at the tomatoes, scallions, beans, radishes, sausages, and sliced ham. After he got his load he was expected to step back to the bar and contribute another ring to the cash register. You could eat and drink very well for fifteen cents.

There were free lunches served that were famous all over the town. The buffet of the Hotel Knickerbocker paraded a marvelous collection of snicks and snacks on its free-lunch counter. The lunch counter actually had chicken salad, lobster salad, lobster Newburgh, melted cheese on toast, cold corned beef, Virginia ham, and even chafing dishes. Unfortunately the beer in the Knickerbocker café was ten cents a scoop. This outrageous price was resented by the better class of lunch grapplers, who seemed to consider a five-cent glass the standard price. The Waldorf, Biltmore, and Plaza hotels all supplied free lunches to their bar patrons, and this method of distributing rations seriously interfered with the restaurant business.

Thousands of bachelors subsisted entirely on the free-for-all banquet style of feeding. However, it was then impossible for a man to bring his family into the barroom and have a basket picnic. Rector's didn't suffer much from the two-beer dining. We had no barroom, and if we had had, we would have been too smart to give away lunches to prospective patrons. The man who lived on free lunch was the same kind of citizen who will look at a circus procession but will never pay to see the circus itself. He lived from hand to mouth—and got most of it on his vest.

The competition among saloon proprietors grew very keen in their individual efforts to attract bar flies by spreading tremendous repasts on the lunch shelf. The buffets with the most free groceries usually got the biggest play from the crowd. A man could get a New England boiled dinner and two beers for ten cents. It got so bad that six or seven of us restaurant owners had an emergency meeting to decide on ways and means of combating the free-lunch evil.

America was free and united in those days. The lunch was free and the cigar stores were united. We decided that we couldn't find anything in the Constitution that declared generously donated food to be aiding and abetting the enemy, and therefore treasonable. So we adjourned the meeting and went over in a body to the Knickerbocker and sampled the lunch ourselves.

The High Cost of Free Lunches

There is a prosperous restaurateur on Broadway today who admits that he acquired all his knowledge of marketing, cooking, and serving food from his early efforts to keep his saloon lunch up to the recognized standard in the old days. He says he actually expended $500 a week in supplying charitable provender for his customers and installed a kitchen to roast the meats. When prohibition came he was thoroughly equipped to change his sign and his business overnight. He now overcharges for his free lunch in an effort to reimburse himself for all the food he handed out to the beer hounds free of charge. I met him the other day and he said that if he finished life with $50,000,000 he would consider himself even. I think that he has no kick coming, as he got rich selling the stuff he used to give away.

Free lunch reached its most magnificent proportions and glory in the city of Chicago. This was in the days when the immortal Hinky Dink sold a twenty-eight-ounce glass of beer for five cents, including an extra lunch without charge and the choice of sleeping on a table or in the sawdust. Twenty-eight ounces of beer is three ounces more than the commercial quart. It was all beer, because foam weighs nothing. But beering in Hinky Dink's was not without its hazards, as the vagrants who infested the place had some unique methods of securing their suds without expense. They would wait until a patron ordered a beer, and the minute he turned his head the boys would drop very thin pieces of rubber hose into the big glass. Then they would siphon the beer out. When the patron turned his head back to his glass it was only to discover that the entire contents had evaporated in transit.

But the place I started to tell you about was Harding's. Harding had a bar exactly 129 feet long, with twenty bartenders operating day and night. There were five extra men on the free-lunch counter and Harding spent $200 a day on his free lunch. There was nothing in New York to approach this lavishness. Lucullus himself could have dined with Lucullus in this place.

Rector's was connected with free lunch in a very direct manner. One of our patrons complained that any man who had picked up a dinner check in Rector's would be compelled to live on free lunch for the rest of the month. Our charges may have been a trifle high, but were not to be compared with the prices of to-day. If a man wants to dine frugally nowadays he must go to a feed-and-grain store and do his best. There is no more free lunch. In fact, as I have explained, there never was. You always had to buy the customary two beers before you could stuff yourself like a turkey on Thanksgiving. The hobo who tried to crash the lunch without purchasing the schooners which came sailing over the bar was generally grasped by a husky bouncer and streeted. The process of being streeted meant that you were grasped by the slack of the trousers and the back of the neck and tossed out on the street. Sometimes the uninvited guest turned the tables on the bouncer.

I once saw a burly hobo sneak into Silver Dollar Smith's, a saloon famous for its shining floor of mosaic composed of Uncle Sam's bright dollars. He made a balk motion toward the bar to fool the proprietor and then turned to the lunch, where he wolfed down the entire exhibit, which consisted mostly of American cheese, Schweitzer, and Limburger. He had all the cheese stowed away before the boss woke up and started for him. The hobo grappled the proprietor and tossed him back over the bar. He did the same thing to the bartenders and then threw the bouncer through the window. With all opposition removed, he then proceeded to chase out the patrons and drank their deserted beer. Completely refreshed and invigorated he watched the owner and his three assistants struggling to their feet and read them a fine piece of advice.

He said, "Don't think that men are mice because they eat cheese."

The most pathetic figure I ever saw fishing for bait at a buffet lunch counter was Davy Johnson, who gambled millions away and had spent hundreds of thousands in Rector's. Davy was the owner of the famous Roseben, one of the most consistent winners on the old-time tracks. Roseben was the original Big Train and was noted for his ability to carry terrific weights and win. Roseben was a sprinter and Davy made $500,000 betting on him before the bookies took a tumble to the Big Train's ability. They soon made Roseben a prohibitive odds-on favorite, and the handicappers seemed to take delight in packing tremendous weights in Roseben's saddlebags. But Davy still continued to bet heavily on his horse, and never batted an eyebrow, even though he may have had $100,000 on his sprinter.

The Big Train in Politics

As Davy said himself: "I went through the bookies like a fox through a henhouse. Roseben won so often that the layers soon made him a top-heavy favorite. Instead of betting one to win two, I had to bet two to win one. But any time I needed $25,000 all I had to do was to put up $50,000, and it was like a rich kid in college writing home to his old man for money. Roseben always got my letters, and what's more, he always answered them. He was a four-legged banking institution."

All the money Davy won on the Big Train was scattered on less reliable investments. He gambled on everything and anything. He would bet that sugar wasn't sweet if he thought the odds attractive enough. His biggest bet was on Judge Augustus Van Wyck to trim Theodore Roosevelt for the governorship of New York State. Davy had $90,000 in cash on election day. He placed that on Van Wyck not knowing that Roosevelt was a human Big Train.

Then he went to Sam Emery, who was his partner in a gambling house on West Forty-fourth Street, just east of Broadway. He sold his half interest in the establishment to Sam for $80,000, which he immediately slapped down on Van Wyck. He now had $170,000 on his political choice. He still had about an hour's leeway before the polls closed and he raised another $30,000, making exactly one-fifth of a million on Van Wyck, whole hog or none.

At eleven o'clock that night Davy knew that Van Wyck had been defeated and his money lost. He didn't have one red penny left to rub against another. He said, "Well, it goes easier than it comes." Then he laid himself down on a couch and slept like a baby until morning. Roseben had passed the peak of his form, and there came a time when the Big Train went to the siding to stay.

Davy was through when Roseben was through. The next time I met him he was at the free lunch. He had lost that Midas touch which turns other people's guesses into personal profit. He was a square gambler, if such a thing exists, and gave his money away right, left, and center. He lived long enough to hear that expression, "He was a good guy when he had it," lengthened into, "He was a good guy when he had it—but he never had it," by a newer generation of gamblers who had never heard of Davy Johnson. His epitaph is the same inscription that has been chiseled over the graves of all followers of the ponies: You can beat a race, but not the races.

My intimacy with big gamblers was due to the fact that I fed them. Rector's was the uptown office for downtown brokers, the city home for the suburban horse crowd, and an anchorage for the ships that passed in the night. It was a Quaker meeting house without the Quakers. Every city had its Rector's in the old days, where society mingled with the mob on the eves of big sporting events. The Parker

House in Boston, the Planter's in St. Louis, the Brown Palace Hotel in Denver, and the St. Francis in San Francisco were temporary mailing addresses for the crowds trekking overland to see big football games, historic fights, or racing.

Just Between Friends

The Palmer House in Chicago was the gathering spot for political leaders who swung the old conventions by the horns.

Washington had its Harvey's, Philadelphia its Green's Hotel, where Fitzsimmons and Corbett almost fought a title bout when they met accidentally in the dining room; and New Orleans still boasts of the old St. Charles, mentioned many years ago by Harriet Beecher Stowe in *Uncle Tom's Cabin*. I don't remember whether Simon Legree or Little Eva stopped at the St. Charles, but it wasn't Topsy.

When the crowd flowed west to see the Kentucky Derby they made the walls of the Seelbach in Louisville ring with the jolly hysteria of folks who expected to augment their fortunes by having a good bet on the winner. The winners and losers gathered the next night in the Phoenix at Lexington, paying off or collecting. The Sinton Hotel in Cincinnati was the Mecca for society and its hangers-on who attended the Latonia meeting just across the Ohio River in Kentucky.

The most brilliant and fairest of the track hotels was the old Manhattan Beach during the days of racing at Brighton Beach. The dining room echoed to the brasses and reeds of Gilmore's Band, which was later supplanted by our own John Philip Sousa. With all due regards to the ultra-saxophonists and super-drummers of to-day, there never was a man who could triple-tongue a silver comet like Jules Levey of Gilmore's Band. He tooted The Last Rose of Summer and left out the thorns. When he played

Shadows on the Water you could hear the little rivulets lapping the sands under the weeping willows.

I forget who danced the night before Waterloo, but when you went to Saratoga you danced every night for thirty nights in either the Grand Union or the United States hotels, and every night was a Waterloo. These hotels are probably the oldest in the land, having been erected around Civil War times. Presidents, princes, and proletariat have stopped there, and they are built on old-fashioned liberal plans which allowed plenty of elbow room for sweeping moustaches resembling the handle bars on bicycles and also dancing space for the hoop skirts of the '70s.

Each covers an immense area, with a patio inside the four walls. Venerable elms with girths like aldermen tower in the patio, and I can still hear the music of Arthur Pryor's Band playing the Blue Danube and see the couples dancing among the mighty elms.

These hotels had quite a problem in running expenses, as they were open only one month out of twelve. The month of August is their big season and must show a harvest sufficient to carry them through the other eleven months. I never could obtain a reduction in rates from the hotel manager, even though I thought a shearer of lambs should recognize the profession. The manager, Leland Sterry, was a good friend of mine, and I managed to even up things whenever he got careless enough to venture into Rector's. I have stopped at hotels all over the world, studying food and service, and the Saratoga hotels stand supreme and solitary in my memory, despite the fact that I have made the grand tour from Petrograd to Nice, from Berlin to Constantinople, and from Baden-Baden to Worsen-Worsen.

The month of August brought the wealth and beauty of the world to the hotels of Saratoga. It was Rector's toughest season of the year. Our business depended on sight-seers and drop-ins, as all the regulars were upstate in Saratoga. They started for the northern race course with bank rolls that looked like heads of lettuce and came back with pockets as empty as Tara's halls. But when October came, with its camphored breezes and crisp profits, we again assembled our quorums and proceeded to run the frivolous business of the nation in a serious way.

There doesn't seem to be any place like Rector's today, where the crowd gathered to discuss events of the day and trade scandal for rumor. Like many of the old-timers I have been set out in the pasture to graze for the rest of my natural days and am out of touch with events; but I am unable to find any set spot where the bankers, actors, and authors assemble for a chat over the chafing dish.

There may be places in cities where the élite still congregate and welcome the newcomer with shouts and banging of spoons on tables as they did in Coffee Dan's in San Francisco, but I am unable to discover any of them. Their place has been taken by the cafeteria and the quick-and-sudden lunch room. Sentiment has been supplanted by business and the long-drawn-out conversation over the coffee and cigars has been discarded for small sales and quick profits. You rush into a restaurant, pick out a table which gives you a safe survey of your hat and overcoat, and proceed to nibble your food in the presence of a thousand strangers. There are four seats at your table, and all four diners are strangers to one another. Even the waiters change from week to week and no restaurant proprietor seems to realize the value of a personal following.

Sacred to the Memory

Rector's never changed its waiters from year to year, because our patrons would have resented their absence. In all my years of catering to the crowd I never sat a man down at a table with a stranger. No man had to keep a vigilant eye on his overcoat and umbrella like a World Series pitcher watching a runner on second base. If I had Aladdin's lamp I would make it into a tail light and try to throw a beam back into the vanished years just for one look at the old days when men were men and waiters were polite.

You could have the next thirty years of my life if you could give me back the thirty that have just elapsed. Or if you can give only one night of the past in return for the thirty years I will give you, I would pick out the night that I stood alone in the new Hotel Rector and George M. Cohan patted me on the back and said, "I'm going to live in your hotel. . . . Rector's has always been a great little place. . . . I'm going to live here by the year. You're a great little guy. So am I."

Chapter 14

Lots in a Name

When George M. Cohan moved lock, stock, and barrel into the Hotel Rector he did us a great favor. The Broadway crowd swung in back of him and soon the same old eggs were roosting in the same old nest. Our bankruptcy was inevitable because of the immense carrying charges of the mortgages which we used instead of shingles on the roof. Like the bulldog which tackled the marble statue, we had bitten off more than we could chew.

Cohan's presence kept us going for five years, and then my father called me into his office one afternoon and told me that the builders of the hotel had announced that they were in and we were out. We were using defeat for a mirror. We stared it right in the face and it had halitosis. The interest on the mortgages was due, and having the walnut in the forceps, the builders proceeded to crack it. They cracked us along with the walnut, and my father retired to his estate on the Shrewsbury, where he died inside the year. It wasn't the loss of his fortune that affected him, but the blow to his pride. He died of a broken heart. Some people are gaited that way.

Knowing that the play called *The Girl from Rector's* had placed a gypsy curse on the hotel, the new owners changed the name immediately. It was up to me to keep the name of Rector before the public; but like many other business men in the same quandary, I was walking Broadway without a dollar. My creditors would have been forced to utilize Madison Square Garden for their indignation congress, while my debtors could all have found standing room on one soap box without crowding. I was willing to take any job connected with the catering game, for I had started in the kitchens of Paris and I was willing to start all over again. The break came inside of two months. I was attending the annual sale of race horses in Madison Square Garden, and during the spirited bidding on The Abbot, a famous trotter, I walked over to get a sandwich at a stand run by Harry Stevens, who has since become the wealthiest caterer in the country. He started selling peanuts in the ball parks and proved there was no easier method of making money without resorting to counterfeiting. He was busy slicing a roast turkey when I strolled over, and I will say that Harry was chipping the meat very thin. The bidding on The Abbot had reached $8,000 and was jumping by leaps and hundreds. Vernie Barton also was purchasing a turkey sandwich and was looking in between the slabs of bread in an effort to discover the turkey, which looked like a very small infant in a very large bed. Then he asked Stevens the price of the sandwich just as $14,000 was bid on The Abbot.

"The sandwiches are a dollar apiece," said Stevens, meanwhile sharpening his carving knife—which was too sharp already.

Just then a bidder shouted, "Fifteen thousand for The Abbot."

Barton took a look at Stevens, then glanced at the auctioneer, and reaching into his pocket, cried, "I will lay $500 at ten to one that the turkey brings more than The Abbot."

The big laugh that followed almost broke up the auction. I got into conversation with Barton and he asked me what I intended doing. I told him I was trying to obtain a lease in Times Square with the view of opening up another Rector's. He introduced me to two young fellows who were standing there and told us to get together. I discovered that the two strangers were seeking to acquire a lease on a restaurant property at Forty-eighth Street and Broadway occupied by the Folies-Bergère Café, which was in bad shape.

The told me they had already sounded the lessee of the building and he wanted $45,000 a year for the place. They thought if I threw in with them on equal one-third shares they could use the name of Rector and chisel the lessee down to their terms. Although I knew one of my future partners but very slightly, and the other was an absolute stranger, I was in a position where a wet straw is a life line, and I was grabbing at anything. All I needed was financial backing and I knew I could make good all over again.

The three of us interviewed the owner of the lease and he tumbled for the name of Rector. He was perfectly willing to switch his demand for $45,000 a year and accept a proposition which gave him 15 per cent. of all beverage sales and 5 per cent. of the food sales. There is such a thing as being too smart. We three wise guys were as brilliant as the boy who was so dumb that his folks had to burn down the schoolhouse to get him out of the second grade. For six years we paid him an average of $100,000 a year instead of the $45,000 he asked originally. But none of us realized what a tremendous thing it was going to be. We got the lease on our own terms, closed the Folies-Bergère for alterations, and opened up in six months under the name of Rector's.

My name was again on Broadway in electric lights on a sign seventy feet high. I strutted around as proud as a wasp with two stingers. We had a magnificent opening night and New York scrambled for a chance to jam their elbows into the first New York restaurant to open as a deliberate cabaret. Our jubilation was, very sweet and short. The builders who had foreclosed on the Hotel Rector procured an injunction restraining me from using the name of Rector in the theatrical district.

We went into court and got a stay, pending the appeal. We continued to use the name of Rector, even though the builders claimed it was a breach of the good will which they had displayed when they squeezed my father and myself out. I called on the opposition's lawyer and he told me that he was empowered to dicker with me for the purpose of getting me to withdraw my name from the new restaurant.

More Noise Than Nourishment

Provided that I pulled out of the triple partnership and never used the name of Rector in New York, he had full authority to offer me the sparkling sum of $5,000 a year. I told him that wouldn't keep me in snuff money and that I never used snuff. He then informed me that he would procure a court order stopping me from using the name of Rector. I told him to go ahead.

Meanwhile our restaurant had picked up speed and was grossing sums we had never dreamed of. The case went to court and the judge appointed Egerton Winthrop as referee. His decision was against us. We immediately appealed the case to the Appellate Division of the Supreme Court and got another stay, pending appeal. We were jumping from stay to appeal like a goat leaping from crag to crag. The name of Rector's continued to burn up the current in electric lights and we were turning away big crowds every night.

I waited on a party of gentlemen one winter evening and saw that they received special attention. One of the gentlemen questioned me about the place, and thinking that he was a stranger in town, I answered all his queries very cheerfully. Our legal contest was almost due for a decision. When that decision was handed down a week later, it was in our favor! The gentleman who had asked me about the methods of running a restaurant seating 1,500 people was the supreme court justice who reversed the opinion of the referee.

He, personally, got a view of me overseeing the place; the testimony proved that I was a legitimate one-third partner and that there was no attempt to delude the public by trading on a name made famous in another establishment. There was nothing to do but to grant me the use of my own name. Esau was entitled to his birthright and his pottage also.

The legal entanglements had no direct effect on our place, as we were open all the time and busy piling up a momentum that was difficult to handle. But Rector's was entering on its final phase, as prohibition also was gathering plenty of speed and was just around the corner.

I speak of the last years of Rector's with regret. Not that it was closed, but because it was ever opened. It was not a restaurant, but a madhouse. We did not delude the public about the name of Rector's, but we hornswoggled them on every other detail. Some 1,500 people paid a cover charge of one dollar a head for the privilege of parking themselves on our hard chairs. They jammed, fought, and tore to get inside. When they got inside, they sat there and wished they were home.

They got nothing for their $1,500 cover charge except noise. That trumpet of brass-bound racket, the saxophone, had just begun to get popular.

Our first orchestra was famous for its endurance and volume. The laughing trombone struggled for honors with the muttering tuba, while the clattering cymbals beat time for the trap drummers and the snares. The sputtering cornets violated all traffic rules when they opened up their exhausts in the city limits. We topped this cake off with a nice icing of robust sopranos and tortured tenors. Bedlam was nothing. This was a twin Bedlam. The craze for dancing with meals was just sweeping the nation, and in Rector's we had an institution that was a new broom. We cleaned up to such a startling extent that our first year's profits paid off our initial investment of $200,000 and left us another $100,000 to divide.

The class of people who patronized the last Rector's was absolutely different from anything I had ever met. All they wanted to do was dance, and we accommodated them with a dance floor that measured thirty feet by twenty. The entire 1,500 all tried to dance on this postage stamp at the same time. The diners would drop their knives and napkins the minute the orchestra broke loose, and stampede for the dancing area. It looked like an elephant dancing on a butcher's block. The couples were jammed back to back, elbow to elbow, and cheek to neck. They resembled the famous drove of horses at the country fair. When the farmer pulled one horse out of the middle, all the rest fell down. They had been leaning on the one in the middle.

There was no space for the old-fashioned waltzers and two-steppers to fling the light fantastic brogan or whirl the nimble rubber heel. The dancers just pulled and tugged, with the result that dancing became obsolete and substitutions were the vogue. Hence the turkey trot, the bunny hug, the fish walk, the Teddy bear, and the Texas tommy.

We had four orchestras playing in relays and they all played like mechanics repairing a locomotive. It was the start of the jazz age, which seems to have aged everybody. Nobody went into Rector's to dine. We had a kitchen, but the chefs were all out on the dance floor with the customers. The waiters danced with the coatroom girls and the maids. The world was not yet safe for democracy and democracy was never safe for the world.

Epicures are complaining that jazz has ruined the art of dining. No man can eat a quiet luncheon in a boiler factory and it is impossible to carry on a conversation on the Tower of Babel. There was a time when the old patrons of Rector's had dined to the digestive lubrication of soft string music, but in the new Rector's we had no soothing and digesting strains from the strings of the harp and the cello. The only things stringy about the last Rector's were the steaks and chops. The worse we grew, the bigger crowds we drew.

Our waiters were renowned for their intelligent insults and our captains for their dexterity in hustling indignant diners to the doors. Sometimes I felt twinges of conscience when I looked around at the idiotic panorama, but I forgot them when I checked up my share of the plunder. I had nothing when I started the last Rector's. I invested absolutely nothing in it but the name, and my income was now $70,000 to $80,000 a year. All I wanted was five years of this and I would be as heavily greased as a Channel swimmer.

We never had any singing waiters, but we had other songsters just as bad. Owing to the terrific noise of 1,500 diners, we had no use for mezzo-sopranos trained on birdseed. Our soloists were picked out for their ability to run the hay scales and register on seismographs. It was a burlesque restaurant and was run strictly on the circus plan. I have never seen anything quite so bad. But the mob kept growing bigger and thicker, until we finally were complimented by the city, which presented us with a city fireman who had orders to whistle for help during the minor panics.

A peculiar feature about the dance hound is that he wants to hop until exhausted and then watch others dance.

This led to the professional cabaret entertainers who specialized in eccentric contortions. A good single performer could always build up a tremendous following. So could a double team consisting of a lady and gentleman. The younger generation will remember the Marvellous Millers, man and wife, who delighted them with whirlwind dancing.

We were always on the outlook for teams, and one night my scouts reported there was a fine couple gyrating daily at the Café Martin—pronounced Mar-tan. I investigated and discovered that Martin was paying them $300 a week, which I considered too much money. I also thought their ballroom dancing was a little too refined for the boisterous atmosphere of Rector's. A month later I offered them $500 a week and they refused. A year later my two partners tried to get them for $2,000 a week and were turned down.

Terpsichorean Teams

This team, reading from left to right, was Vernon Castle and his wife, Irene, who I consider had more individual influence on any one nation than any woman with the exception of Joan of Arc. Even at that, Irene was the Joan of Scissors, for she popularized the boyish bob worn by every young girl and the girlish bob affected by every old girl.

Maurice and Florence Walton were another pair of dancers who had a tremendous vogue about this time. Mae Murray, the movie star, was dancing in Murray's cabaret, which boasted of a revolving floor upon which dancers skidded and wabbled. Rector's never had a revolving floor, but we supplied the nectar of the keg which produced the same circular effect.

The Marvellous Millers were with us a year and then left on a vaudeville tour. We were anxious to engage some team to fill the terpsichorean gap, but could find no one with a big enough name. One night a peculiar individual shuffled into Rector's, smoking a big cigar that was ablaze from stem to stem. It was the most amazing cigar I have ever seen. It spouted sparks like a Roman candle and seemed to have an all-rubber wrapper with a blended soft-coal filler.

This exotic person wore a derby hat that looked like the hood of the first motor car, and his green and red sweater was illuminated by a big horseshoe pin studded with precious bits of glass. His trousers were tight and displayed the muscular grapefruit development of his bulging knees. He aimed his cigar at me, and must have pulled the trigger, for I was soon gasping for breath in the finest cloud of smoke I have ever seen outside of the B. & O. tunnel under Baltimore.

He said, "D-do you run this j-j-joint? Or don't y-you w-want your j-joint c-called a j-joint?" I told him I was one of the three proprietors, and he replied, "I'm a d-dancer when I don't t-talk. I w-want to show you my st-st-st-stuff."

To the Stage Via Rector's

He was a dancer when he didn't talk and make no mistake about that. His name was Frisco, which name he had appropriated from a west-bound box car. His home was in Dubuque, Iowa, and he had arrived in New York via Chicago, where he had danced in the Loop j-j-joints. He showed us his st-stuff that same night, walking out on the dance floor without any other makeup than his street costume, which proved to be just right.

New York had never seen any dancing like Frisco showed it that evening. We were so delighted with his instantaneous success that we gave him what he asked—exactly f-fifty dollars a week. He was with us five months and then jumped to $1,500 a week in vaudeville. He is now the only stuttering monologist on the stage and reckoned as one of Broadway's wits.

His most famous stunt happened in front of Rector's one morning about three. He came out of a coffee-and-waffle armory with a bag of crullers and started to feed the soggy quoits to a scraggy horse attached to an ice wagon. A copper strolled up and asked Frisco what he was doing, whereupon Frisco replied, "I w-want to see how many c-crullers he can eat be-before he hollers for a c-cup of c-c-c-c-coffee."

Rector's was the proving ground for ambitious performers. As fast as we trained them, the stage grabbed them. Frisco was responsible for the advent of another favorite—Ted Lewis, who makes the clarinet sit up and whimper. He wasn't satisfied with the tempo furnished by our hit-and-run orchestras and we finally selected Ted Lewis to swing the baton. Ted made good from the jump. Inside of a week he was a separate attraction. Rector's also developed the Mosconi Brothers, who have danced in every theatre in the country; but our biggest card was a Metropolitan Opera contralto who started in Rector's under the name of Miss Edwards. She is right on top now with a name culled from the gardens of Bulgaria. I will not pronounce it, Frisco cannot, so her secret is safe.

Cabaret entertainment was the direct result of the dwindling ability of people to amuse themselves. It marked the ending of the old-time restaurants with their quiet atmosphere and subdued lighting. We whispered across the candle lamps in the old days. But now a conversation must be pitched one octave higher than a bellowing, howling saxophone in order to be heard. When the music is thumping along its rough roadbed, it is possible to whisper sweet nothings—provided you have a megaphone big enough. Every person at the table is now a cheer leader. The most important article of evening clothing is the ear muff. The Autocrat of the Breakfast Table has been succeeded by the Maniac of the Cover Charge.

Chapter 15

THEN CAME THE WAR

The first year of Rector's was the noisiest I ever experienced. But I hadn't heard anything yet. A man by the name of Von Kluck started on a detour to Paris and the war broke out. Or, if you prefer it in your daily movie-title style, then came the war. New York was flooded with European agents buying battle confetti. There wasn't a single room to be had in any hotel and the theatres and cabarets were jammed nightly. We were forced to build an annex to our amusement sanitarium.

Although America was not to toe the scratch until three more years had come and gone, the battle spirit seemed to prevail. Wages jumped high, tastes leaped higher, and prices looped over the moon. We stepped our cover charge up to two dollars a plate and it was paid cheerfully. Everybody made plenty of money and spent it as if the magic pocket would never grow empty. It was the golden era for the working man who had always longed to mingle on Broadway, and he proceeded to take full advantage of it. His wife wasn't satisfied with dancing in the evenings, but also desired the afternoon dance. This is where the *Thé Dansant* made its appearance along with the flapper and the lounge lizard.

Rector's hired another crew of waiters and laid in a fresh stock of orchestras equipped with sound-proof trombones, and thoroughly qualified to scramble the seven notes of music into a fine omelet. This *Thé Dansant* business was a laugh for cabaret owners, but it was a terrible thing for the American home. The ladies would arrive about three in the afternoon and were not fooled by the name "*Thé Dansant.*" Neither were we. It was a booze dansant, even though the cocktails were served in fragile Dresden china teacups. The women had started on their march to suffrage and emancipation by acquiring a flair for strong drink in the afternoon.

A good time was had by all. After a drink or two, they would naturally want to dance. As the majority of ladies were unescorted, their lawful breadwinners being engaged in the pursuit of earning a living, it was up to Rector's and the other afternoon resorts to supply dancing partners. In the absence of breadwinners, we furnished cake eaters, and that's how that word started.

Cake Eaters and Lounge Lizards

These cake eaters were the original lounge lizards, who toiled not, but did spin on the dance floor. We supplied them with their meals and gave them a wage of about fifteen dollars a week. It was a legitimate industry for good dancing men, and many actors worked in the *Thé Dansant* as male hostesses. Quite a few of them rose to fame, the most important being Rudolph Valentino, whose dancing in *The Four Horsemen* made him a star. He was an expert in the tango, which was just beginning to become popular with the older ladies who had an ear for music but no foot for tempo.

These old-timers loved their "tea," but had reached that age where dancing partners are difficult to get. Most of them were fat and ponderous, but insisted on dressing like flappers, with short skirts, painted faces, and bobbed hair. One, especially, was a work of art, and if perfection is youthful beauty, she had it, for she didn't have a wrinkle in her rouge or a gray hair in her toupee. She can be best described as mutton done up as lamb.

Incidentally, the *Thés Dansants* were responsible also for the sudden growth of beauty parlors in the big cities and the fine decorative work now being done on faces. This was the period when it was impossible to tell whether a man was escorting a new wife or an old one painted over. The *Thés Dansants* were very lucrative for cabarets, Rector's alone averaging $1,000 an afternoon and more at Saturday matinées, when the suburban college girl came to town to complete her education.

These incredible conditions lasted through 1914, 1915, 1916, and just when reformers thought they must get better, they got worse. America entered the war and old manners and customs were contraband. Rector's acquired some of its old-time brilliance. Strange uniforms were seen on the dance floor, mingling with the overseas khaki of the American soldier and the overseeing blue of the American home guards. The bright breeches of the French aviator, the comfortable kilts of the Black Watch, the Sam Browne belt of the English officer, and the dusty brown of the Anzac crusader bobbed and weaved in the new dances on Rector's floor.

The cake eater and the lounge lizard went into the Army and came back to Broadway for one last fling with the orchestra, tanned and lean from the summer and fall in the first training camps. There was a weird aroma of patriotic hope and fear in the atmosphere. Hilarity led its ace to dull care only to have it trumped by hysteria. In all my career as a restaurateur I have never seen such sincere drinking, such sustained jollity, such Marathon dancing. We were forbidden to serve drinks to American soldiers and sailors, and they resented the fact that our Allies were permitted to guzzle all that their skins could hold. This resulted in many pitched battles on the dance floor, until I was convinced that the war was being won by Rector's bouncers.

The incident which sticks out clearest in my memory is seeing our inebriated door man refuse admission to a Scotch kiltie because the short-skirted Scot didn't have an escort with him. Only a basso roar from the Gordon Highlander convinced the door man that the Scotchman was no lady.

The playing of the various national anthems was always good for a Rectorian battle. No matter whether it was the English, French, Chinese, or American battle music, there was always some person who refused to stand up during the rendition. Sometimes a pacifist would refuse to arise during the playing of our own anthem. Bingo! The fight was on. Fists would fly two, four, and twenty at a time. Over in the corner, surrounded by women and soldiers of all the armies, was the celebrity known as the Wolf of Wall Street. He would order wine for everybody in the room. One treat alone stood him $800. He carried $20,000 and $30,000 in his pockets at all times and never started an evening that he couldn't finish.

Ling Rector Foo's Place

No American sailors or soldiers were ever served drinks after we got our orders, but the boys circumvented the rules by going down to Coney Island and coming home soused to the gills. Investigation by secret-service men as to how soldiers were served drinks in uniforms revealed that the boys went to Coney Island, hired bathing suits, and proceeded to get plastered in the Boardwalk saloons. Then they would doff the nonreg bathing outfits and roll home happily in the G. I. uniforms. After that, every bathing suit issued to an enlisted man had a big U. S. on it, front and back.

Then wartime prohibition came along, and after a consultation with my partners, in which we could not agree on policy, I sold out to them for a considerable sum and the stipulation that the name Rector should come down from the front door and the roof. I walked out on the restaurant game in June, 1918, and on January 1, 1919, the Rector griffin came down forever, after exactly twenty years on Broadway and almost a century in Lewiston, Lockport, Chicago, and New York. Although there is—or was—a Rector's in London, it was no branch office of ours. I understand there is also a Rector's in Paris and one in each of the main cities in this country. Neither my father nor myself ever gave them permission to use the name, but you cannot stop a man from calling his dog Rover. The name seems to be a charitable one that covers a million culinary sins.

The percussion cap that exploded the old flintlock happened in Maryland. I was driving through that hospitable state one day and saw a big green-and-red electric sign sparkling over a Chinese chop-suey foundry. Wiggly yellow snakes chased one another around the borders of the sign and in the center was the biggest "Rector" in lights I had ever seen. I went in to see the celestial proprietor and asked him how he got the license to use the name.

He said, "In Chinese, my middle name is Rector. I got plenty right to use name. Nobody can stop me. That's my middle name."

This made my middle name in Chinese something like mud. I guess that the middle name Rector is still using his Chinese translation. We never tried to stop him after his legal explanation. The name figured so largely in theatricals that it was carried all over the country and grew familiar to thousands who never came down out of the hills. Every musical show had some reference to our place. Probably the best known was the one used in Weber and Fields reviews.

In a conversation between a woman and man, the fellow said, "I found a very valuable pearl in an oyster."

The girl retorted, "That's nothing. I got a diamond from a lobster over in Rector's last night."

The biggest single bit of free advertising we ever got was from a young playwright named Gene Walter. Gene had written his first play and carried it from producer to producer. They all turned it down, and in desperation Gene took it to David Belasco, who had already refused it twice. This time Belasco was in a receptive mood and consented to give the play a trial performance. The name of the piece was *The Easiest Way* and it was one of showdom's greatest successes. The final scene was between the heroine, Frances Starr, and the hero. As the last curtain fell on the break-up between the two, she sat on her steamer trunk and said, "You go to hell. I am going to Rector's."

A Popular Road House

They not only wrote, spoke, and sang about the old-time restaurants but they also composed poetry in their honor. One of the best—in fact the best—was written to a rival restaurant by Langdon Smith, then sports editor on the old *New York Herald*. One verse of the poem, which is on love through the ages, reads:

> And that was a million years ago,
> In the time that no man knows;
> Yet here to-night, in the mellow light,
> We sit in Delmonico's.

Delmonico had the poem printed on the backs of all his menus in spite of the last lines, which ran:

> And as we linger at luncheon here,
>   Over many a dainty dish,
> Let us drink anew, to the time when you
>   Were a tadpole and I was a fish.

We would hardly call Delmonico's customers fish, especially in the present meaning of the word, which classifies a fish as one who is entitled to have his name inscribed on that famous roll of honor, the Sucker List. Rector's also had its place in poetry, even though we must stretch the word a bit and include the rimes which are made when the doggerel is barking. Clarence Harvey sat down one morning after a rather hazy evening in Rector's and wrote the following poem to his lady love, of which numerous verses I recall only the last:

> And we motored down to Rector's,
>   Where all was gay and bright;
> And by the way, dear empress,
>   Who took you home that night?

If you will pardon the eccentricities of an old-timer who is reaching a rheumatic arm down into the grouch bag of the past, I want to say that nobody sings about the restaurants of the present, and if they do, they do all their singing on complaint blanks. The art of dining has truly degenerated, and all that people seem to remember of the rules of health is that an apple a day keeps the doctor away while an onion a day will keep everybody away. I am out of the restaurant business for good, and I guess patrons of the last Rector's will all shout "Good!" I apologize to them for the manner in which we shook them down for the privilege of squeezing into the place, but it must be blamed on the war.

When I cleaned up at the end of five years there was $250,000 clinging to my mud guards. I thought I was fixed for life, retired to the suburbs, bought a home, a flivver, and a cow, and proceeded to live quietly. I had a cellar stocked with legitimate pre-war combustibles and my Jersey cow supplied me with butter and milk. The first three days in the country were serene and beautiful. But when Saturday night came a horn tooted outside the door and I opened it to find an old friend there. I welcomed him heartily, wined and dined him and gave him godspeed, with instructions to come back soon. He did—and brought another friend.

Before the month was out I discovered that I was in the restaurant business again, but this time without profit. My friends literally ate me out of house and home, and three years later everything was gone except the cow—and she was dry. So was the cellar. Home entertainment is a serious matter these days, and 1 advise all young couples to place good brake linings on their household budgets.

To Insure Poor Service

The quickest way to the poorhouse is to travel too fast away from it. By this I mean trying to live beyond your means in an effort to convince neighbors of your success. It is all right to entertain, as a guest at the supper table puts everybody on his good behavior and forestalls the usual small bickerings which feature the average home supper. We cannot deny that most of our quarrels are over the dinner table. This is because the husband has been at his office all day, the wife has been busy with her own household affairs, and the evening meal is the only chance for her to unburden herself of the woes of the afternoon. I advise all couples to dine out at least twice a week. Pick out some good sensible restaurant which doesn't boast of its home cooking. That's exactly what you are trying to get away from.

Laughter is the best aid to digestion. Don't criticize the food or argue with the waiters. If the meal is bad you only make it worse by fighting. Retire gracefully and never go back to the same place. One chronic grumbler at the table can spoil everybody's evening. It is possible to have a lot of fun in a bad restaurant if you can get into the mood. I remember Smith and Dale, of the Avon Comedy Four, playing their restaurant scene. It has been greeted by typhoons of laughter by audiences for more than twenty-five years and is still running in its original form without a line being altered. Smith is a very bad waiter with his finger in everything. Dale watches him bring in the well-thumbed soup and various dishes and finally orders: "Bring me a whole coconut and try to get your thumb in that."

When Smith brings in the whole coconut, the audience sees that he is carrying it like a bowling ball. He has bored two holes in it. Dale orders sweet milk. Smith shouts back to the chef, "A glass of milk—and it shouldn't smell from herring." Dale's request for hash results in Smith yelling into the speaking tube, "Sweep up the kitchen!"

And when Dale protests against the size of the bill, Smith assures him that the place is run just like Rector's. I have seen that act many times and it always rolls me over into the aisle. If I ever get back into the catering game, I assure you that Smith will be one of my waiters. He would keep all my diners in good humor, and that is the most important feature of a meal. Irritation and spleen are the keystones of stomach trouble and modern after-dinner speakers are cashing in on their ability to make banqueters laugh.

Smith would make a fortune as a waiter, because Luke Barnett has been doing the same thing for years. He is an invaluable addition to any feast as he arrives dressed as a foreign waiter and then proceeds to wreck the evening. He works out of Pittsburgh and has travelled all over the world in his specialty.

Alexander Moore, former Ambassador to Spain, was the first to realize Barnett's possibilities at a home dinner. Mr. Moore introduced Barnett into his home as the new butler and he proceeded to buttle. Mrs. Moore, who was Lillian Russell, was entertaining some very distinguished guests that night and was horrified when she saw the new butler serving the soup out of a coffeepot. However, thinking that none of the guests had noticed it, she kept silent, but arose in indignation when he got into an argument with a guest whom he accused of throwing olive pits on the floor.

Food and Fist Fights

Mr. Moore smoothed that difficulty out, but no sooner had the guests sampled the fish than Barnett snatched the dishes away and served another course. A lady about to harpoon a salad with her fork never stabbed anything but the cloth, for Barnett had everything timed and grabbed the dish before anything could be eaten. He kept the table in a well-modulated uproar and the night culminated in a fist fight between Mr. Moore and his new butler, who was floored three times, much to everybody's delight. An aged diplomat, who was so feeble that he couldn't spoon his mashed potatoes, stood on his chair and shouted, "Good, Mr. Moore! I was just going to do the same thing myself."

A big laugh followed when Barnett was fired by Lillian on the spot, and he left, only to come back and shout through the door, "I resign." It was only then that Lillian realized that she had been hoaxed, and she immediately hired Barnett for a dinner the following week. He has worked banquets in New York, Newport, Southampton, and all the Florida hotels.

The newspaper publishers will remember him when he impersonated a Polish editor at one of their national dinners in New York. He actually spoke in imitation Polish for thirty minutes in defense of President Wilson's Fourteen Points, and gained the sympathy of the audience when he broke into tears at the finish.

Bad News for Business Men

Jim Corbett brought Barnett on for a dinner at the Friars Club, and he arrived with full credentials as a captain of waiters. Some 800 banqueters were having a solemn, peaceful time when Barnett got into his inevitable argument with Frank McGlynn about throwing olive pits on the floor. Mr. McGlynn is the very fine actor who created the role of Abraham Lincoln in John Drinkwater's play of the same name. No more quiet man than Mr. McGlynn ever lived, but he remonstrated when Barnett asked, "What kind of sloppy business is diss? Vere you think you are—home?"

Other guests rallied to the famous actor's support and testified that he had never thrown an olive pit on the floor. Barnett spouted another long speech in artificial German and wound up by blowing a whistle and calling fifty waiters off the floor. The trouble wound up in a fist fight between Corbett and Barnett, and the fake waiter was again floored, much to the enjoyment of the diners, who thought he was getting what he deserved. The evening continued with Barnett enthroned on the dais between Corbett and William Collier. But the fifty waiters never did come back. They imagine to this day that they were participants in a general strike called by an authorized walking delegate.

Of course, Smith and Barnett are outside of my general talk about Rector's, but I cite them to indicate the importance of jollity with meals. This idea was carried too far in the New York restaurant, for the professional entertainment soon outdistanced the cuisine. The man who wanted music with his meals was fortunate if he got any food with his music.

Never go into a cabaret expecting to get good food. Wait until you find a restaurant proprietor who eats in his own place. It will be safe for you to eat there, too. The medicine must be pretty good if the physician takes it himself. As I said once before, the main trouble with American dining is that we wolf our food. Nature gives you thirty-two busy little ivory anvils in your mouth and you should use them all.

The great French chef, August Escoffier, who has just finished a visit to America, says that we should spend at least two hours on the big meal of the day and an hour for breakfast. That will be news to the commuter who grabs his breakfast on the run like a coyote raiding a henhouse. I am a gulper myself, with the result that I am as bloated as a little blimp. I know it is wrong, but I have acquired the national habit of snapping at my food in the mistaken idea that if I don't hurry I will miss the news reel at the movies.

It has been a real pleasure for me to have had the privilege of writing this haphazard review of the life of *The Girl from Rector's,* because it has resulted in renewed friendships with many of the old patrons of our Forty-fourth Street establishment and brought back memories of what we fondly call the good old days, when a pedestrian was considered every bit as important as a citizen, when lovers eloped on bicycles, and a well-dressed woman looked like a boarding-house hat rack with all the boarders home.

They may have been good old days for some people, but I prefer the electric light to the sulphur match; I would rather have the radio than the squeaky melodeon; and when I travel I shall take the fast express and wave out of the window as you rush by behind faithful old Dobbin.

The good old days are a deception invented by ancient fogies who want to exaggerate without running the danger of being checked up on their statistics. If they want to add six inches of snow to the big blizzard of 1888, let them do it, so long as they allow us to grab a shovel with them.

Pleasant Memories

Rector's was an institution while it lasted, but it outlived its vogue. Jack's, Delmonico's, and the others are also hull down on the horizon and only the watcher in the crow's nest of memory looks in vain for their return. When they departed they left a gap that closed up like a pinhole in rubber. A little air of reminiscence escapes from the puncture as it has done in these reminiscence but the tire rolls on just the same.

I have enjoyed writing this stuff, because it has helped to renew old acquaintances and revive fond memories. This has been my first adventure with a recipe that called for facts and anecdotes instead of parsley and garlic. I have enjoyed it; for, after all, we live in the past, and no doubt the bullfrog, with his powerful back legs, often thinks with regret of the fine flipper he used for a propeller when he was a tadpole.

And now I am something like the old actor who made the best of his first and only opportunity. After a lifetime spent in trying to get a star part on the stage, he finally engaged passage on a liner and jumped overboard in mid-ocean. The crew managed to turn the spotlight on him, and, like him, I will take my first and last bow and go down for the third time.

About the Author

It would not be out of line to refer to George Rector (1878-1947) as one of America's first celebrity chefs. He came from a family of restauranteurs, with his grandfather operating hotels with restaurants in New York State. Rector's father, Charles, opened a dining room in Chicago, which became the popular Rector's Oyster House. In 1899, Charles and George opened Rector's in New York on Broadway. Though working in the restaurant, George was also studying law, but his father sent him to France for training in the Café de Paris. During the early 1900s, iterations of Rector's continued to be among the most popular restaurants in New York City, only ending upon the coming of Prohibition. George Rector wrote several cookbooks and a popular cooking column for the newspapers, had a weekly radio program (*Dining with George Rector*), and appeared on television and in at least one movie (*Every Day's a Holiday*, 1937).

See also:
ANATOMY OF A RESTAURATEUR: GEORGE RECTOR
https://restaurant-ingthroughhistory.com/2018/07/11/anatomy-of-a-restaurateur-george-rector/

Rector's, New York City, 1899-1919
https://www.theamericanmenu.com/2015/08/rectors.html

Rector's: The Elaine's of 1899
https://www.toquemag.com/uncategorized/rectors-the-elaines-of-1899

Also Available // CoachwhipBooks.com

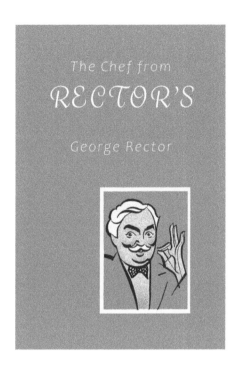

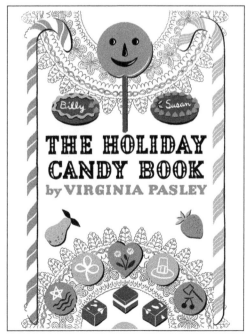

Also Available

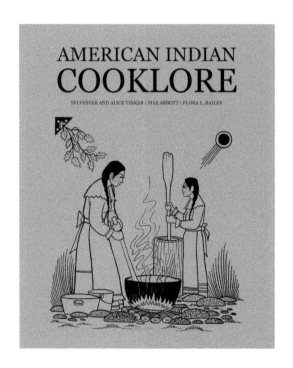

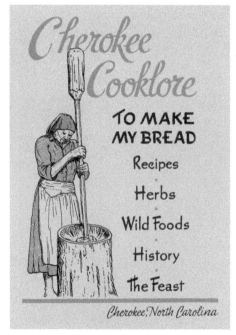

CoachwhipBooks.com

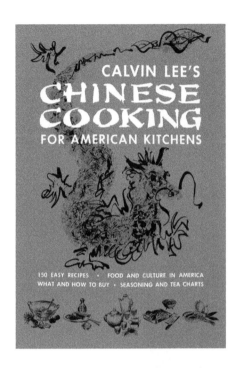

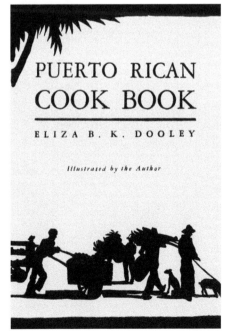

Also Available

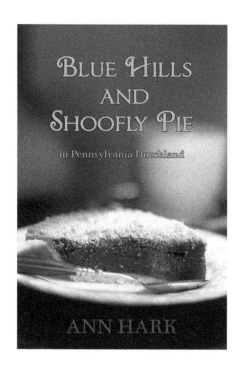

CoachwhipBooks.com

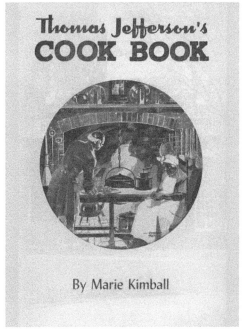

Milton Keynes UK
Ingram Content Group UK Ltd.
UKHW041828201024
449814UK00001B/234